Mommy It's a Renoir!

ART POSTCARDS FOR ART APPRECIATION

A PARENT AND TEACHER HANDBOOK

by Aline D. Wolf

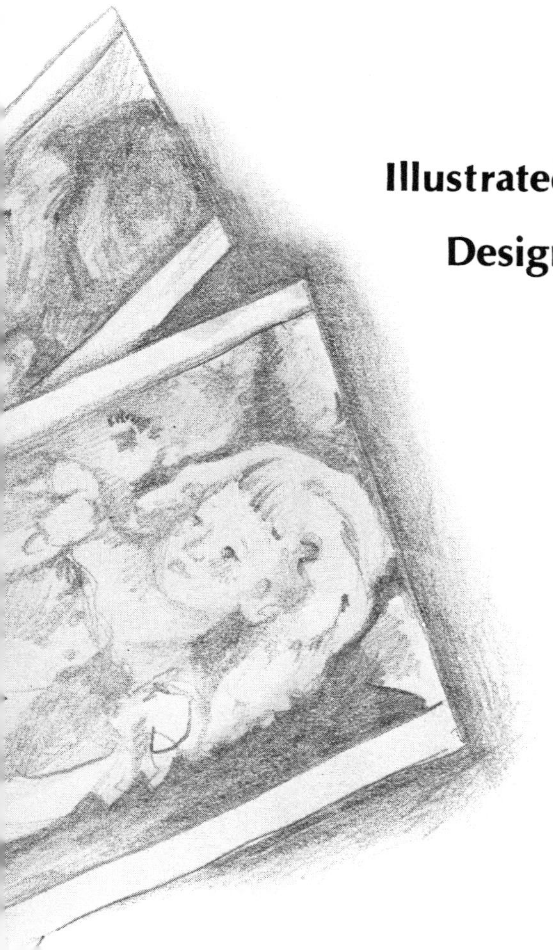

Illustrated by JANINE SGRIGNOLI WOLF

Designed by Joan Stoliar

PARENT CHILD PRESS

Altoona, Pa.

Dedicated with love to my sons and daughters—

George	Patrick	Christopher
Cathy	Gregory	Dorie
Mary	Charlie	Gina

Acknowledgments

Since its inception several years ago, this book has had many special friends who gave me meaningful assistance and enthusiastic support. In particular I wish to acknowledge the contributions of the following people:

My husband, Jerry, whose fabulous art postcard collection was my original inspiration for all the activities described here, and whose cover photographs and constructive criticism contributed significantly to the finished product;

My assistant, Peggy Curran, who patiently typed several revisions of the manuscript and aided me throughout the project with her competence and skill;

Special friends, Paula Benjamin and Dr. Marilyn Goldberg, whose editorial assistance greatly enhanced the clarity of the text;

Artist, Joan Stern, and art historian, Thea Blake, who each reviewed the manuscript with her particular expertise;

Teachers, Grace O'Connor, Dr. Ann Marie Swartz, Betty Niles and Marie Hale who evaluated the manuscript in terms of its application to classrooms;

Shamim Rajpar and Bonnie Sell who took photographs for the cover;

Art critic, Victoria Donohoe, who graciously contributed the foreword;

Dorie Wolf, Mary and Bill Martone, Wendy Pyle and Elaine Grinthal who read the manuscript in progress and offered helpful suggestions.

This book would not have been possible without the beautiful illustrations drawn by my daughter-in-law, Janine Wolf. I deeply appreciate her graciousness in preparing many more illustrations than we had originally planned.

And, finally, I wish to acknowledge the vital role of the designer, Joan Stoliar, whose enthusiasm for the entire project inspired her to combine the text and illustrations in a most artistic and practical format.

My thanks to all the above as well as to many others who gave me encouragement and valuable comments during the long period of preparing this book.

A.D.W.

Foreword

The cultural gap is an unavoidable part of the modern landscape, ever since the vital tissues were cut that kept artists securely bound to society centuries ago. Artists gradually achieved liberty for self-expression and declared themselves independent of the art patron. But they paid a high price for it, namely isolation and to some extent alienation.

One way we have today of bridging that gap modestly is by art reproductions—straightforward, no-nonsense ones that have some amount of authenticity but do not mislead by claiming to be exact facsimiles. Postcards top the list of such plainspoken, widely available art reproductions.

Postcards have universal appeal. Significantly, although aimed directly at the mass market, their impact goes far beyond it, perhaps more so than any other type of art reproduction. Avid postcard enthusiasts include countless artists, among them some of the foremost painters of our day. Many of them fasten favorite art postcards to their studio walls and easels. Also, numerous art students and art professionals (myself included) can tell you that, as teenagers, they built large collections of art postcards stored in shoeboxes. Enthusiasm for art postcards at any age enriches a person's life. We are certain it is having this effect if it sharpens, not dulls, our appetite for first-hand contact with art originals.

The author of this book, Aline D. Wolf, believes that this enrichment experience through art postcards can begin in a child's earliest years. Her insights, both as a mother and teacher, prompted her to question the lack of art appreciation activities in early learning programs. Why, she wondered, did adults constantly offer the cute and the mundane to children who had the potential to savor the genuine, the finely detailed and the truly beautiful. In her opinion, youngsters could savor such quality if it was a part of their everyday experience.

In *The Process of Education*, the cognitive psychologist, Dr. Jerome S. Bruner, wrote, "The task of teaching a subject to a child at any particular age is one of representing the structure of that subject in terms of the child's way of viewing things." Aline Wolf applies this dictum to art appreciation. Because of her extensive experience in Montessori education, she sensed that pre-schoolers would never browse through an encyclopedia of art but that they would delight in selecting two drawings by Rembrandt—an elephant and a lion—and placing them side by side. Not original drawings, of course, but postcard-size reproductions which are so comfortable in the hands of children.

Mrs. Wolf has developed a unique series of graduated art postcard exercises which she describes clearly in this manual. In doing so, she has demystified elementary art appreciation so that it can be handled by the neophyte adult art lover. I welcome this exciting publication to the art world and I appreciate its outstanding merits and usefulness.

Victoria Donohoe
Art Critic, *Philadelphia Inquirer*
and *Knight-Ridder Newswire*

Preface

This book is for parents, teachers or any other adults who want to experience the delight of introducing beautiful paintings to young children. It describes an art postcard project which my husband and I began informally at home with our own children and which I later adapted for use in pre-school and early elementary classrooms.

In more than one way this project departs from the traditional methods of teaching art appreciation. It invites adults who are not necessarily art specialists to present fine art reproductions, in a simple way, to children who have not yet reached the age usually considered appropriate for this subject. And it dispenses with the "Please do not touch" directive which normally accompanies the study of fine art. In all the activities the children handle the postcard-size reproductions.

Children as young as three can do the beginning exercises. The succeeding steps gradually increase in difficulty and are appropriate for each child's level of experience rather than his or her specific age.

I have found that many of these activities are suitable for children with handicapping conditions, particularly for deaf youngsters who find an unusual joy in working with the postcards. In fact, art postcards are appropriate for all ages. Over a long period of time I have shared my collection informally with teen-agers, adults and elderly citizens who enjoyed doing the exercises to test their own knowledge of paintings as well as to meet the work of artists whom they had not previously encountered.

The emphasis in this project is on exposing young children to art reproductions rather than filling them with the facts of art history. Therefore no formal art appreciation courses are necessary for parents and teachers who are presenting art postcards to children. Basic information, such as the title of the painting and the artist's name, are printed on the reverse side of each card. In addition, Part Three of this manual contains further reference material for readers who desire it.

The difficulty of writing for a broad audience of adults is that the details essential for some readers are not necessary for others. Experienced pre-school or elementary teachers, for example, will not need some of the explanations in Parts One and Two, while art history experts will already be familiar with much of Part Three. In the interest of enabling any reader—involved parents, creative grandparents or any other caregiving individuals—to share this art project with young children, I have included all details necessary for doing so.

I particularly want to offer some encourage-ment to those readers who may hesitate to under-take the project because they feel inadequate in the subject of art. Many years ago when I was answering our own youngsters' questions about the art postcards, I had to refer constantly to the information printed on the reverse side of the cards. After a relatively short time, however, I was able to recognize the style of many artists; I could guess their names before turning the cards over. "Do you know this one, Mommy?" my children would ask. Sometimes I didn't know and the children seemed comfortable with the fact that I was learning too.

So if you have a gnawing feeling of inferiority whenever art is discussed, don't worry. You will learn in an easy and delightful way, as I did, when you start buying, sorting and sharing art postcards with young children.

A.D.W.

The art postcards which appear in this manual are the illustrator's renderings of well-known paint-ings which are usually available in postcard-size reproductions. The black and white drawings are intended to give you a sense of the original paintings so you can visualize the various exercises which are described. The real postcards which the children will use when doing the exercises are full-color reproductions of the original paintings.

Contents

CONTENTS:

STEP 1 MATCHING IDENTICAL

LEVEL 1
EASIEST

Children as young as three can match identical pairs of art postcards. They begin with a few pairs that are easily distinguished from each other—totally different in subject, color and style. While matching, the children become familiar with beautiful paintings.

LEVEL 2
INTERMEDIATE

Here the identical pairs have some similarity to each other in either subject, color or style. In order to select identical pairs children must look more carefully at the details of each painting.

STEP 2 PAIRING COMPANION

LEVEL 1
EASIEST

Children delight in finding two examples of an artist's work that are similar but not identical. Initially each companion pair is radically different from all other companion pairs. Therefore children use subject clues to distinguish the companion pairs of one artist from another.

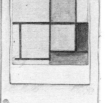

LEVEL 2
INTERMEDIATE

The difficulty is increased when the subject matter of one companion pair is somewhat similar to the subject matter of other companion pairs. Children now use both subject and style clues to distinguish the companion pairs of one artist from another.

PAINTINGS

LEVEL 3
ADVANCED

There is an even greater challenge when all the identical pairs are by the same artist and feature the same subject matter in the same style and color tones. Here children compare fine details in order to match the identical paintings.

page 34

AINTINGS

LEVEL 3
ADVANCED

All the companion pairs have the same subject matter and some pairs have color tones similar to other pairs. Therefore the children look at the artist's style as the principal clue for pairing two particular paintings.

page 42

CONTENTS:

STEP **3** GROUPING FOUR PAIN

LEVEL 1
EASIEST

Initially the four paintings of each artist must be very similar to each other and radically different from the four paintings of the other artists. Children begin by using subject clues to select four examples of a painter's work.

STEP **4** LEARNING THE NAME

In this activity, children can see one subject as it was painted by several well-known artists. By referring to control cards and then putting artists' name cards below their paintings, beginning readers can gradually learn the names of important artists.

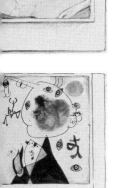

LEVEL 2
INTERMEDIATE

Here the four paintings of each artist are similar in subject to the four paintings of each of the other artists but radically different in style. Children use obvious style clues to select four examples of an artist's work.

LEVEL 3
ADVANCED

Here the four paintings of each artist are similar in subject and also somewhat similar in style to the four paintings of the other artists. Children must notice fine differences in style to select four examples of each artist's work.

OF THE ARTISTS

CONTENTS:

STEP 5 LEARNING THE NAME

After referring to control cards, children can place both title and artist cards below particular paintings. With this activity young readers learn the titles, as well as the names of the artists, of some of the world's most famous paintings.

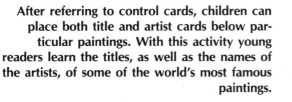

STEP 6 LEARNING ABOUT TH

A small folder is used to hold several examples of paintings from each of the important schools of art. Children can become aware of the characteristics of the paintings in a particular school of art and learn the names of that school's most well-known artists.

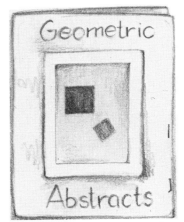

OF FAMOUS PAINTINGS

The Age of Innocence
by Reynolds

The Age of Innocence

by Reynolds

CHOOLS OF ART

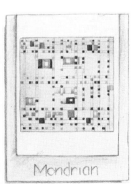

Mondrian

Malevich

Noland

CONTENTS:
STEP 7 GROUPING PAINTING

With this fascinating sorting exercise, children learn to distinguish one school of art from another. At Level 1 they sort three schools that are radically different from each other. At Level 2 and Level 3 the children sort paintings from schools whose characteristics are more similar.

STEP 8 USING A TIME LIN

Children can place art postcards beside their appropriate dates on a Time Line to form a visual representation of the sequence of developments in painting. After learning the technique by first making a Time Line of his own life, a child can then use a larger Time

F ART

Line to locate particular artists and schools of
art in their places in history. Time Lines enable
children to see a graphic illustration of the
evolution of painting from pre-historic cave
paintings to the abstract paintings of the
twentieth century.

page 64

PART ONE
Art and Young Children

HOW THIS PROJECT BEGAN

One day when our youngest child, Gina, was six years old, she asked if she could help me open the mail. I gave her a few of the envelopes which had arrived that day. When she opened the first one she became wide-eyed. "Mommy," she said with great excitement, "it's from Renoir!"

In her hand was a lovely note card. On the front of it was, indeed, a beautiful print of a Renoir painting; inside was a letter, not from Renoir, of course, but from a close friend.

Whenever I tell this story, I am immediately asked, "How did she know it was a Renoir when she was only six?" At the time I did not think it was remarkable that she recognized a Renoir because for about two or three years, she and her older sister and brother had been playing with our collection of art postcards. We allowed them to do this in the evenings before they went to sleep. Usually they would spread the postcards on our big bed and pick out the ones they liked. When they found a particular favorite, my husband or I would tell them the name of the artist. Sometimes we would show them another painting by this same artist and they would put the two postcards side by side. It became a game. "Can you find a Picasso?" we would ask. "Do you see another one that you think was painted by Miro?" or "Let's put all the Mondrians on the pillow." Because Mondrian's technique of using geometric shapes was so distinctive, his was one of the first styles they were able to recognize.

After several months of playing with the postcards, looking at them, putting them in groups, asking questions and making quite original comments about the subjects, the children were able to identify several of the artists. So I was not surprised when Gina recognized the Renoir; I was only charmed by her assumption that he was writing a letter to us.

Our young children's enthusiasm for art postcards contrasted dramatically with the half-hearted interest that our older sons and daughters often displayed toward art appreciation courses in junior and senior high school. As I reflected on this contrast, I was inclined to believe that the pre-school years, when children are so fascinated by picture books, are the more naturally sensitive years for them to become familiar with paintings. Adults are constantly showing young children pictures of apples or farms or families. Why not also show them a lovely still life by Cezanne, a fine landscape by Corot or a beautiful mother and child by Mary Cassatt?

As I watched our own children's delight in playing with the art postcards at home, I began to think that any pre-school or early elementary classroom could be enriched by such a collection of cards. Because my professional experience was in pre-school education, I could visualize using art postcards in simple classroom exercises, based not on formal art appreciation lessons, but on the activities similar to those our children had enjoyed at home. During the ensuing years, I experimented extensively with art postcards, designing and evaluating the exercises which are described in Part Two of this manual. Readers who are familiar with the work of Maria Montessori will recognize that some of the structures I have used are similar to those that Montessori formulated for teaching botany, geometry and history to young children.

How Young Children Learn

Before using these exercises at home or in the classroom, it might be helpful for adults to reflect briefly on the unique way in which young children learn. When you observe children closely, you will notice that their style of learning is quite different from the way we learn as adults. As an example, consider the way a two year-old acquires his native language. If he is not speech handicapped, he can almost unconsciously absorb any language or languages he hears spoken as he simply goes about his daily routine. Compare this effortless process with the way an adult must struggle to learn a foreign language—memorizing vocabulary, imitating accents, studying grammar etc.—and you will understand the difference in these two styles of learning.

During the years when a child is assimilating language, he is constantly absorbing other information from his environment as well. Depending on where he spends his time, a child automatically takes in and remembers details of the kitchen routine, farm animals, neighborhood life, TV characters or whatever other situation he frequently experiences. This fact places a rather awesome responsibility on any parent or teacher who is the caretaker of a child's environment. By carefully selecting what is actually in the environment, the adult can enrich the child's experience during the years when he has this special aptitude for effortless learning.

Cultivating Taste

Fine taste in the arts, or in any aspect of life, cannot be specifically taught nor suddenly acquired. It develops slowly and subtly as a result of frequent exposure to examples which various cultures and generations have recognized as significant.

The earlier this exposure occurs, the more likely that genuine taste will become truly a part of a person's nature. A man who grew up on a horse-breeding farm, for example, possesses instincts which enable him to recognize the superiority of a particular horse whose fine qualities are not obvious to average onlookers.

Adults who are new to appreciation of art are like onlookers. They say, "I like this" or "I don't like that," but their judgment is not formed by experience and their joy and appreciation are limited. Whenever they attempt to determine what is valuable and lasting, they must depend on their gut reactions or the opinion of others.

By introducing children to fine art at a young age, we give them the opportunity to develop a taste for genuine quality from their earliest years. A print of a beautiful painting, hung in the kitchen at the eye-level of small children, will become as familiar to them as peanut butter and jelly. A variety of paintings in their early classroom experience will enhance their awareness of the great diversity in art and entice them to further discovery. Fine details in art give much pleasure to those who can perceive and respond to them. Therefore, I believe that by bringing art into the everyday environment of young children, we, as parents or teachers, have the opportunity not only to awaken their appreciation of beauty, but also to expand their capacity for joy.

Displaying Art Prints in the Child's Environment

A large selection of various size prints are available at a nominal cost from many museums. Expensive framing is not necessary. You can protect a print by placing it on a piece of equal size heavy cardboard, wrapping both in clear plastic and fastening the plastic with tape on the back. Or you can use a flexible frame—heavy cardboard and a piece of glass held together with small clamps.

A few well placed paintings are more effective than a large collection hung in every available space. If you look carefully at your environment, you will easily find three or four good locations. Prints can be hung on either side of the classroom door or on the child's bedroom door at home. They can be hung on any low wall space, on the ends of shelf units, on the side of an upright piano, or on the side of a chest of drawers. Smaller size prints can identify a child's coat hook, work basket, laundry basket, file folder or notebook.

It is interesting, but not necessary, to coordinate the subjects of some of the paintings with various classroom or household activities. Paintings of children reading create a delightful atmosphere near book shelves or on the walls of a reading corner: *Girl Reading* by Pablo Picasso; *The Fairy Tale* by Walter Firle; *A Young Girl Reading* by Fragonard. Renoir's *A Girl With A Watering Can* is a perfect reminder for a child to water the plants. There are many beautiful paintings of still life that are appropriate in a dining area or near a snack table and Rembrandt's *Girl With A Broom* goes well with classroom practical life materials—brooms, mops, carpet sweepers—or on the door of the broom closet at home.

One year in September, I hung an 8″ X 10″

Because of this experience and other similar ones I urge you not to change your art prints every week. Let them hang for several months at a time so that the children can "soak up" the details. It is not necessary to explain paintings or to make them the subject of a formal lesson. I have always felt it is not quite fair to tell the child what you like about a painting. Good art speaks for itself! Simply hang the painting where the child can see it and let the absorbing process happen. After the painting has been in the environment for a while, the children will, in some way, indicate to you how it has impressed them. They may even point out a detail that you have overlooked.

reproduction of Picasso's *Child With A Dove* on the outside of one of the doors in the school hallway. I placed it on the lower half of the door, so both the preschoolers and the primary grade children could see it every day on the way to their classrooms. It hung there all year because somehow we never got around to changing it. Toward the end of the school year, one of the seven year-olds, without any urging from anyone, made a free-hand drawing of this picture. It was a remarkably good copy. We realized that, as she approached this door day after day, she had without any particular effort absorbed a detailed impression of this lovely print.

Why Use Postcards?

If children can absorb art appreciation from prints displayed in the environment, then why have art postcard exercises? The answer lies in the fact that children learn a great deal more from materials which they can handle than from those which they can only see.

Paintings on the wall are usually not to be handled or moved by children. The same is true of prints in large expensive art books. If adults show such books to youngsters, they usually caution them not to touch, which to the children means not to experience fully. In other words, they are denied the "doing"—their most natural means of reinforcing their visual impressions.

Young children by nature love to use their hands. In fact, when we observe children carefully, we notice that they have an uncontrollable urge to handle everything in sight. They want to pick up and examine each new object they encounter. They are frustrated if, placed in an environment of dangerous or fragile objects, they are constantly told, "Don't touch." This command actively counters one of their strongest natural tendencies.

It seems that information enters children's brains through their hands as often as through their eyes. The renowned educator, Maria Montessori, based her manipulative learning materials on her belief that, "The hand is the chief teacher of the child." Hands not only gather information for children they are the means by which children work through that information, verifying it and reinforcing it.

It is important, therefore, for children to handle some art in their environment. I believe that art postcards are ideal for children's activities because they are inexpensive, child-size, light weight and readily adaptable to many different methods of displaying, comparing, sorting and storing.

Caring for the Postcards

Permitting young children to handle postcards, however, in no way implies that they should be allowed to abuse them. These reproductions represent some of the greatest treasures of various world cultures and, as such, should be handled with appropriate respect. Although the postcards are not expensive, it is not always convenient, or even possible, to replace them. It is important, then, from the very beginning to show your children how to use the postcards with care.

Your own attitude toward the art postcards will be the key to the manner in which the children respect them. Before you introduce the postcards, you might tell the youngsters that in a few days you are going to have a very special project for them. This project will have beautiful pictures painted by famous men and women from many different countries. You will impress the children even more if you let them see that your hands are clean before you handle the cards. Then ask each child to check her hands before beginning the project. When handling the postcards yourself, do so slowly and deliberately. Shuffling them roughly or stacking them carelessly might indicate to the children that the postcards are not really as special as you say they are.

Keeping the Postcards in Order

I insisted that order be an inherent part of this project because I believe that young children learn best in an orderly situation. Contrary to what many adults presume, children are actually more comfortable with orderly procedures in an orderly environment than they are in an atmosphere of chaos. A youngster who must wade through a cluttered playroom with broken toys all over the floor usually does not have significant or happy play experiences. Consequently a child's experience with art postcards can be meaningless if he is simply given a shoe-box full of cards and allowed to scatter them all over the floor.

In Part Two, I describe the order that will give meaning to your postcard collection—order in the way the cards are arranged, order in the way they are stored and order in the way they are used. Once the children become familiar with your orderly routine, even the youngest of them will be comfortable using the cards. In fact, they will probably complain if they find that some postcards are not in their usual place or if they see another child using the postcards in a way that is different from the regular procedure. The children will maintain the order in this way only if you establish it before bringing the postcards into their environment.

Programming the Activities for Success

In my experience, children derive the greatest pleasure from art postcards if an adult first prepares the postcards by grouping them in particular exercises for the children "to do." Just as a set of blocks of graduated sizes can invite a child to build a tower, a set of postcards, purposefully pre-selected can intrigue a child into a delightful learning activity. You, as parent or teacher, can prepare such exercises in advance, following the instructions in Part Two of this manual.

The sequence of the exercises actually programs the child for success. The first activity—

matching three identical pairs of postcards—is so simple that it is almost impossible for a child age three or older to fail in doing it. After this initial success, the child is challenged by a new exercise, not too different from the one just mastered, but containing an additional degree of difficulty. The series then continues with a gradually increasing variety of paintings as well as a gradually increasing challenge in the tasks that the child is asked to perform.

Attracting the Child's Interest

Even though I have pre-arranged the order in which you present the postcards, I suggest that you follow this order in a relaxed, non-structured time-frame. In other words, never pressure a child to do the project. It is not a formal course with lesson plans, deadlines and tests. Rather it is an enrichment project that is most effective when, and if, the child chooses it freely.

The adult's role, therefore, is to intrigue the children, not to force them to work with the postcards. Do this by attractively displaying your postcard project within the reach of the children and by letting them watch you demonstrate the activities. When you are showing the children how to do the little tasks, do so slowly, at the pace of a child, and rely on your actions more than your words. It is easier for children to imitate the actions they observe than it is for them to translate your verbal instructions into performance.

Attracting children to this project is not difficult. In my experience, whenever a young child first observes an adult or another child using the art postcards, the on-looker will nearly always say, "Please, let me do it next!" The project literally sells itself to pre-schoolers.

So let each child come to the project and work through it at his or her own pace. Some children will show more interest in the postcards than others because one child naturally differs from another in interests and preferences. Some will work more quickly than others. Some will delight in repetition of the simplest exercises even after they can do the more advanced steps, often because repetition is the best means of reinforcing their experience. Or they may return to these initial activities because they are comfortable with the tasks they can do easily or because they like to look at some particular paintings in the beginning exercises. Do not let this repetition of simple exercises cause you concern; it actually enables the children to absorb more details of each of the postcards they handle.

The *Eight Steps* described in Part Two can take a child from the simple matching of identical paintings to locating individual artists and schools of art in history. The best time for a child to do each of the different *Steps* depends on his individual development and interest. What one child can do at six another will do at eight and still another at ten. If a "too simple" task is selected by an older or more experienced child, he will be bored. If a "too advanced" task is chosen by a very young or inexperienced child, he will be frustrated. Your job is to carefully sense when a child is ready for each new challenge. When the child responds with delight, you will know you have demonstrated or suggested an activity that is appropriate for his particular stage of development.

PART TWO
Art Postcard Activities

This Part contains complete descriptions of eight types of exercises that can be done with art postcards. Each kind of exercise is called a *Step* and some of the *Steps* are sub-divided into graded levels of difficulty. Small pocket-folders are used to hold the postcards for the activities in each *Step*. For easy identification, I have assigned a particular color to the pocket-folders in each of the *Eight Steps*.

All the pocket-folders within each *Step* are the same color and invite the child to do the same kind of task. For example, all the red folders in *Step 1* indicate matching identical paintings. The number of folders in each *Step* depends on your budget, the number of children you are working with, and their degree of interest in each of the particular *Steps*.

Step 1 *Matching Identical Paintings*—red folders.

Step 2 *Pairing Two Paintings By The Same Artist*—blue folders.

Step 3 *Grouping Four Paintings By One Artist*—light green folders.

Step 4 *Learning The Names Of The Artist*—yellow folders.

Step 5 *Learning The Names Of Famous Paintings*—tan folders.

Step 6 *Learning About The Schools Of Art*—gray folders.

Step 7 *Grouping Paintings From The Same School Of Art*—black folders.

Step 8 *Using Time Lines Of Art*—orange folders.

To prepare each of these *Steps,* you must purchase the postcards, mount them, arrange them in sets and display them. Although this preparation is time-consuming, it affords you a practical opportunity to become very familiar with the paintings you will be using. For me, time actually passed quickly when I became absorbed in the project. Don't try to prepare all *Eight Steps* at one time. Do the work gradually as the children become ready for each new *Step.* When you finish the preparation, you will have created a unique and beautiful set of materials which you can use with children for many years.

Buying the Postcards

Before writing this book I presented this project in lectures to parents and teachers in many parts of the United States. A typical response was, "I love it. But where do I get all the postcards?"

Art postcards are sold in the museum shops of nearly every art museum in the United States and abroad. Most museums feature postcard reproductions of the paintings in their own collection. Only a few include reproductions of paintings from other museums or from private collections. You can, indeed, purchase art postcards at museum shops. But in order to get the variety of cards necessary for the *Steps* in this project, you would have to visit a great number of museums.

Therefore, for your convenience, sets of art postcards which are arranged to correspond to all the *Steps* in this manual have been prepared. Information about mail-ordering these sets can be found on page 96.

Even if you purchase these basic sets through mail order, you will probably want to augment your collection whenever you visit a museum.

There are three points to remember when purchasing art postcards for this project:

1. All the cards in these collections are 4½" X 6" or smaller.

2. When purchasing two postcards of the same painting to be used for identical matching, buy them at the same time so you can be certain they look exactly alike in color intensity and in the portion of the original painting that is reproduced.

3. While it is always tempting to purchase art postcards that are particularly appealing to you, this criterion actually limits the styles in your collection and imposes your taste on the children. A child's preference often differs from that of an adult as well as from that of other children. It seems only fair, therefore, to select postcards representing many of the different styles or schools of art recognized in the art world. Descriptions of these schools of art begin on page 74.

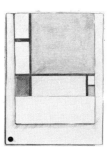

Mounting the Postcards

The best way to prepare art postcards for children's use is to mount each one on a plain background card. The mounting card is used for the following purposes:

1. To serve as a backing to protect the postcards from being wrinkled or bent.

2. To provide a background on which you can put either the color-coding symbols or names required in many of the exercises.

3. To be grasped by the person handling the card, thus keeping fingermarks off the actual postcard.

Complete details for mounting postcards can be found on page 70.

Making the Pocket Folders

The most practical storage for the two sets of postcards to be paired is a 6" X 8" folder with two pockets inside. I recommend this size folder because it is very comfortable for children to handle. As far as I know, this size is not commercially available, but complete details for making these folders can be found on page 71. Parents doing this project at home may prefer a more simple means of storing their postcard sets, such as using envelopes or clear plastic bags.

Arranging Them in Sets

For many of the exercises described here, the postcards are arranged in sets of six which are to be paired or grouped with other sets of six. For *Steps 1, 2,* and *3,* which can be done by children who are not yet able to read, one set is distinguished from another by ¼" self-stick colored dots affixed to the lower left corner of the face of the mounting card. The dots called Color-Coding Labels are available in office supply stores. Please note: In the black and white illustrations in this manual

○ = a yellow dot;

⊕ = a green dot;   ⊜ = a red dot;

● = a black dot.

Printing Names and Titles

In many of the *Steps,* you will have to print names on mounting cards or titles on folders. Before starting this task, select a simple style of manuscript lettering, such as the one illustrated on page 72, and use this same style throughout the project. When printing the name of an artist, use only the last name or the name by which he or she is most commonly known.

The Purpose of the Exercises

The overall purpose of *Steps 1* through 8 is to help young children to develop a simple familiarity with reproductions of fine paintings. The specific tasks in the early *Steps* require the children to look carefully at the art postcards, to notice their details, and to place them in a particular order. The more advanced *Steps* are designed to help the children to learn the names of important artists, to recognize examples of their paintings, and to locate some of them within a particular school of art and/or period of history.

In most pre-school classrooms, children learn to match identical colors, identical shapes, identical pictures of fruit, etc. Because matching identical paintings is simply a variation of these exercises that the children already know how to do, it is the logical first *Step* for this project.

Selecting the Postcards for Step 1

Careful selection of the postcards for each exercise is vital to the success of this project because the actual selection determines the progression of difficulty. In *Step 1* there are three levels of increasing challenge:

LEVEL 1
EASIEST

All identical pairs in a folder are totally different from all the other pairs in that folder, primarily in subject, but also in color and style. Because of the radical differences between each pair in a folder, it is almost impossible for a child who understands identical matching to do the exercise incorrectly.

Magritte
First Love
Private Collection

L PAINTINGS

Materials

- At least three, but preferably six or more, red pocket-folders.

- Yellow and green color-coding dots— one package of each.

- Up to six pairs of mounted postcards for each pocket-folder.

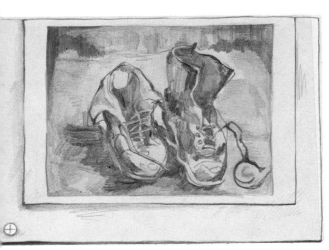

Vincent Van Gogh
Boots With Laces
Van Gogh Museum, Amsterdam

Sir James Guthrie
To Pastures New
Aberdeen Art Gallery, Scotland

31

LEVEL 2
INTERMEDIATE

Some of the identical pairs in each folder are somewhat similar to other pairs in that folder. They can be similar in subject; they can be similar in color *or* they can be similar in style. Because of this slight resemblance between some of the pairs, the child must look more closely at the details in order to make the correct matches.

Pablo Picasso
Le Gourmet
National Gallery of Art,
Washington, D.C.

Using the Names of Artists or Paintings

When introducing art postcards to very young children, it is not necessary to teach the names of the artists or the names of the paintings. You can mention an artist's name casually whenever you sense that his or her work is a particular favorite of one of the children or whenever the child is using a number of examples of that artist's work. But do not burden youngsters with learning names during these early stages. In the first two *Steps* it is sufficient for the children simply to enjoy looking at and pairing the paintings.

The names of many artists are difficult to pronounce. Before using unfamiliar names with the children, check the pronunciation in the Index of Artists on page 92.

John Bradley
Little Girl

Paul Gauguin
Young Breton With A Goose
Collection Armand Hammer,
Los Angeles

LEVEL 3
ADVANCED

All six identical pairs in each folder are very similar to each other. They are all by the same artist; they all feature the same kind of subject *and* they are all done in the same style. This high degree of similarity requires the child to check details very carefully in order to do the exercises correctly. Some examples of paintings which can be used in Level 3 folders are listed here:

Six pairs of blue-green garden scenes by Monet.
Six pairs of many-peopled scenes by Breughel
Six pairs of Cubist paintings by Picasso
Six pairs of misty seascapes by Turner

Since all six pairs in each folder in Level 3 are by the same artist, print this artist's name on the front cover of the folder.

Pablo Picasso
Still Life With Liqueur Bottle
The Museum of Modern Art, New York

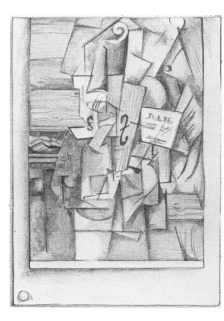

Pablo Picasso
The Guitarist
National Museum
of Modern Art, Paris

Identifying and Storing the Sets for Step 1

1. Place a yellow color-coding dot on the lower left-hand corner of six of the mounting cards, i.e. one card from each of the six pairs you have selected for a folder.

2. Place a green color-coding dot on the lower left-hand corner of each of the remaining six mounting cards.

3. Make sure that the cards with the green dots are piled in a different order, top to bottom, from the cards with the yellow dots.

4. Put the postcards with the yellow dots in the left pocket of a red folder, and place a yellow dot on this pocket.

5. Put the postcards with the green dots in the right pocket of this same folder, and place a green dot on that pocket.

6. Paste an art postcard on the cover of the completed folder. If possible, this cover card should be identical to, or similar to, one of the cards stored in that folder. At least it should be by one of the same artists. Before pasting the cover card, print its title and the artist's name on the back cover of that folder.

7. Label each folder as either Level 1, Level 2 or Level 3.

Pablo Picasso
The Violin
Stattsgalerie, Stuttgart

35

Displaying the Folders

The project is most appealing if the different art postcards on the front of each pocket-folder are in full view. There are several alternatives for display, listed in order of preference:

- Lay the folders, face-up, on low slanted shelves, similar to those used to display magazines in libraries.

- Open each folder slightly and stand it upright on a flat shelf. Place several of these upright folders in a row on two or three low shelves.

- Lay the folders face-up in a row on a long, low flat shelf.

- If your shelf space is very limited, display only a few folders and store the remaining ones in a file sorter or record rack.

Demonstrating Step 1

1. Begin when a child indicates some interest in the folders you have displayed.

2. Sit beside the child at a low table or on the floor. If demonstrating on the floor, use a large plain-colored mat as your working area.

3. Temporarily put aside three of the six pairs from a Level 1 folder and use only the three remaining pairs for your demonstration.

4. Point out to the child that you are handling the cards by grasping only the mounting cards rather than putting your fingers on the postcards.

5. Remove the set of three postcards from the left pocket and lay them down in a vertical row.

6. Remove the set of three cards from the right pocket and place each one beside its identical mate.

7. Point to the two paintings in each pair and be sure the child notices that they are identical.

8. Pick up the postcards in the first vertical row and slide them into the left pocket of the folder so that the identifying yellow dot on the top card is visible above the pocket. Show the child that this dot matches the dot on the pocket, clearly indicating that this pocket is the storage space for the cards with the yellow dots.

9. Mix up the order of the cards in the other vertical row, so that they will not be in the right order for the next user. This maneuver is important here and in all the succeeding exercises, so exaggerate a bit when demonstrating it and explain why you are doing it. Replace this second set in the right pocket.

10. Invite the child to do the exercise with the demonstration folder.

Responding When a Child Makes an Error

1. Don't comment immediately; give the child an opportunity to correct her own mistake.

2. If she doesn't make the correction herself, point to one of the mis-matched pairs and ask, "Does this painting look exactly like that one?"

3. If this question does not lead to a correction, the child may not be ready for this exercise. Wait several months and then try it again.

Gradually Increasing the Challenge

In my experience, however, this first folder in Level 1 is too simple, rather than too difficult, for most children aged three or older. As soon as a child succeeds with it, he is usually ready and eager for a more challenging activity. You can give him this challenge immediately by putting back, one at a time, the three pairs which you had temporarily set aside from this initial folder. When the child can match all six pairs, give him another Level 1 folder for further practice.

Continue this same sequence for Level 2 and Level 3 as the child is ready.

STEP 2 PAIRING COMPANION PAINTINGS

Step 2 offers the children a new and fascinating challenge! In this *Step* they are asked to pair companion paintings—two paintings by the same artist which are *not* identical but which are similar in both subject and style. When doing this exercise, the children cannot look for identical details as they did in *Step 1*. Instead they try to recognize a similarity in two examples of a painter's work. This task is much more sophisticated, but it can be made so simple that even four year-olds can do it.

When establishing a pair of companion paintings, *you* must be able to recognize immediately the similarity in style; otherwise this similarity will not be obvious to children. In other words

don't study the identifying information on the reverse side of the postcards in order to make up a pair. Instead, select two postcards in which you can see a strong resemblance in subject, style and color tones. Then check the reverse side to be sure they are by the same artist.

Many painters, such as Picasso, radically changed their style through the years so that an example of their early work may have nothing in common with a piece from a later period. Take particular care, therefore, to choose for companion pairs two paintings done in the same style, which usually means they are from the same period of an artist's work.

Selecting the Postcards for Step 2   LEVEL 1 EASIEST

Each companion pair must be made up of two vertical or two horizontal paintings. All the companion pairs in one folder must be radically different from each other, primarily in subject but also in style and color.

For example, in one folder you can have the following selections:

A pair of portraits

A pair of landscapes

A pair of still lifes

A pair of abstracts

A pair of flowers

A pair of animals.

Pablo Picass
Child With A Do
National Gallery, Londo

Piet Mondria
Composition, 19.

18th Century Chine
Flowers and Bir
Bibliotheque Nationale, Pa

Pablo Picasso
Le Gourmet
National Gallery of Art,
Washington, D.C.

Piet Mondrian
*Composition with Red
Blue and Yellow*

Materials

● At least three, but preferably six or more, blue pocket-folders.

● Red and black color-coding dots—one package of each.

● Up to six companion pairs of mounted art post-cards for each pocket-folder. Each pair in a folder must be by a different artist.

At this level a child will rely mainly on subject clues to select the two paintings by the same artist. The use of such highly contrasting subjects practically insures his success.

Flowers and Birds
Bibliotheque Nationale, Paris

Beatrix Potter
The Tailor Mouse
Tate Gallery, London

LEVEL 2
INTERMEDIATE

Begining with this level a companion pair can be made up of two verticals, two horizontals or one vertical and one horizontal. The six pairs in each folder are not so radically different from each other as they were in Level 1. Some of the pairs can have similar subjects but should be highly contrasting in style and color. Other pairs can have the same predominent color but contrasting subject matter.

Many combinations of pairs can be used for Level 2. As you work with the project, your experience will soon tell you which assortment of pairs will be gradually more challenging for the children.

For example, in one folder you can have either of the following combinations:

Two highly contrasting pairs of boats

Two highly contrasting pairs of geometric abstracts

Two highly contrasting pairs of flowers

or

Three highly contrasting pairs of animals

Three pairs in which the predominent color is the same but the subjects are very different.

Franz Marc *The Gazelle*
Rhode Island School of Design Museum

Rembrandt
Lion, Boymans-van
Beuningen Museum

40

Beatrix Potter
*The Mice Sewing
    the Mayor's Coat*
Tate Gallery, London

Since some of the pairs in this Level are similar in subject to the other pairs, the child can no longer rely entirely on subject clues when pairing two paintings by the same artist. The color clues are also not so reliable as in Level 1 because two or more pairs in a folder can have the same color tones. Therefore the child begins to look more closely at the style of the paintings when determining a companion pair.

Franz Marc
Sitting Horse

Rembrandt
Elephant
British Museum, London

Pablo Picasso
Pierrot With Flowers

LEVEL 3
ADVANCED

The six pairs in each folder all have the same subject matter. Examples for each of several folders follow:

Six companion pairs of portraits of children

Six companion pairs of abstract paintings

Six companion pairs of paintings of flowers.

The key to enabling a child to do this advanced work is a gradual transition from subject clues to style clues. Because the subjects are all the same in Level 3, the child can no longer use subject clues. Colors, too, are frequently similar when the subject matter is similar. So at this point the child must rely on the artist's style to make the correct associations.

Joshua Reynolds
The Age of Innocence
Tate Gallery, London

Paul Gauguin
Young Breton With a Bucket
Collection Armand Hammer, Los Angeles

42

Pablo Picasso
The Artist's Son
Picasso Museum, Paris

Preparing the Sets for Step 2

1. Place a red color-coding dot on the lower left-hand corner of six of the mounting cards—i.e. one card from each of the six pairs you have selected for a folder.

2. Place a black color-coding dot on the lower left-hand corner of each of the remaining six mounting cards.

3. Put the postcards with the red dots in the left pocket of a blue folder and place a red dot on this pocket.

4. Mix up the order of the cards with the black dots and put them in the right pocket of the same folder. Place a black dot on that pocket.

5. Paste an appropriate art postcard on every folder cover; label them Level 1, Level 2 or Level 3 and display them as you did for *Step 1*.

Joshua Reynolds
Master Hare
Louvre, Paris

Paul Gauguin
Young Breton With a Goose
Collection Armand Hammer, Los Angeles

43

Demonstrating Step 2

1. Use a Level 1 folder containing only three companion pairs.

2. Tell the child that the exercises in the blue folders are different from those in the red folders. In these new exercises she is not going to pair two paintings that are exactly alike, but two similar paintings by the same artist.

3. Place the first set—the three paintings identified by red dots—in a vertical row.

4. Explain that these paintings were done by three different artists—and each of these artists had a special way that he or she liked to paint. For example, if you are using the geometric abstracts by Modrian which have square and oblong blocks of color framed by straight heavy black lines, help the child to become aware of this style by asking questions. "Do you think this artist liked to paint people or shapes? Did he like to use bright colors? What kind of lines did he draw around colors?" etc.

5. Select one painting from your second set— the three paintings identified by the black dots— and tell the child you are looking at the style— the special way it was painted.

6. Try it beside each of the three paintings in the first set and tell the child you are looking for a painting in the first set which is painted in this same special style.

7. The child may point to the correct mate in the first set. If not, you make the decision and place it beside its companion.

8. Pair the remaining cards in the second set with their companions in the first set.

9. Point carefully to each pair so the child will notice the similarities.

10. Put the cards back in the pockets and invite the child to do the exercise with the same folder.

Increasing the Challenge

If you prepare your folders carefully, children as young as four will have little or no difficulty in correctly pairing two companion paintings by each of three artists. As soon as a child can do this, add more companion pairs to this initial folder. Because pairing companion paintings is a totally new task for the child, he will need several Level 1 folders for practice. After he has worked successfully with three or four of these, he can try the challenge of Level 2, and eventually Level 3.

After many years of experience I feel that pairing companion paintings is one of the activities in this project which young children enjoy most. Youngsters, age four through eight, seem particularly comfortable with the challenge of *Step 2*. They constantly ask for new folders, seeking an ever increasing variety of paintings to experience.

STEP 3 GROUPING FOUR

Step 3 is an extension of *Step 2*. Instead of pairing only two paintings by each artist, the child is invited to identify and group four paintings by each artist.

Selecting the Postcards
LEVEL 1
EASIEST

The four paintings by one artist must be similar to each other in both subject and style. At the same time these four paintings must be very different in subject and style from the four paintings by each of the other two artists included in each folder. For example, in one folder you may have the following:

Four paintings of ballet dancers by Degas

Four abstract paintings by Miró

Four paintings by Michaelangelo

LEVEL 2
INTERMEDIATE

The subject matter of all the postcards in each folder are the same, but the styles of each of the three artists are radically different. Following are examples of three folders of portraits you can have:

Four paintings by Mary Cassatt

Four paintings by Michelangelo

Four paintings by Van Gogh

Four paintings by Renoir

Four paintings by Rembrandt

Four paintings by Rouault

Four paintings by Leonardo da Vinci

Four paintings by Cezanne

Four paintings by Carl Larsson

Edgar Degas
Arabesque
Louvre, Paris

Joan Miró
Women and Bird in the Moonlight
Tate Gallery, London

Michelangelo
Head of Libyan Sibyl

AINTINGS BY ONE ARTIST

Materials

- At least six light green pocket folders.

- Yellow, green, red and black color-coding dots.

- Four mounted postcard paintings by each of three artists for each double folder.

Edgar Degas
Two Dancers

Ballerina

*The Dancer With
The Bouquet*
Louvre, Paris

Joan Miró
Dutch Interior
Museum of Modern Art, N.Y.

*Personnages et Chien
Devant Le Soleil*
Offentliche Kunstsammlung
Basel

*Woman and Little Girl
in Front of the Sun*
Hirshhorn Museum
Washington, D.C.

Michelangelo
Head of God the Father

Head of Delphic Sibyl

Head of Etruscan Sibyl
Sistine Chapel, Rome

LEVEL 3
ADVANCED

All the postcards in a single folder have the same subject matter and, at this level, the styles of the three artists are not so radically different from each other as they were in Level 2. In some cases you can provide this increase in difficulty simply by rearranging the postcards you used for Level 2. This new arrangement will require the child to look even more carefully at fine details of style.

For example, you can regroup your three folders of portraits as follows:

Four paintings by Mary Cassatt
Four paintings by Carl Larsson
Four paintings by Renoir

Four paintings by Van Gogh
Four paintings by Cezanne
Four paintings by Rouault

Four paintings by Michelangelo
Four paintings by Rembrandt
Four paintings by Leonardo da Vinci

Preparing the Sets for Step 3

1. Put a yellow dot on the mounting card of one painting by each of the three artists; a green dot on a second painting by each artist; a red dot on the third painting by each artist and a black dot on the fourth painting by each artist.

2. In the space below the painting on each of the mounting cards *in the first set only*—the set with the yellow dots,—print the last name of the artist or the name by which he or she is most commonly known. Do not put any names on the remaining three sets.

Preparing the Folders

Since each folder in this *Step* must accommodate four sets of postcards, it must be a double one, having four pockets.

1. To make this double folder, attach the back cover of one folder to the front cover of a second folder with either paste, rubber cement or staples.

2. Use a yellow color-coding dot for the first pocket, green for the second, red for the third and black for the fourth.

3. Mix up the sequence of each set and then store each set in the pocket with the corresponding colored dot.

4. Paste an appropriate art postcard on the cover; label as Level 1, Level 2 or Level 3 and display.

Demonstrating Step 3

1. Tell the child that when he uses the light green folders he will group four paintings by one artist.

2. Place the first set—the three paintings with the yellow dots—in a vertical row.

3. Remove the second set—green dots—from the folder and place each painting beside its companion in the first set.

4. Remove the third set—red dots—from the folder and place each painting beside its companion in the second set.

5. Remove the fourth set—black dots—and place each painting beside its companion in the third set.

6. When the layout is complete, make sure the child notices that each horizontal row has four paintings by the same artist and each vertical row has three paintings with the same colored dots.

7. Mix up the order of the cards in each vertical row and return them to the appropriate pocket.

8. Invite the child to do the exercise with the same folder.

Using the Names of the Artists

As you will notice in the illustrations for *Step 3*, each horizontal row of four paintings by one artist is impressive. It will give any child, or even any onlooker, a good idea of the style of that particular artist. Therefore, it is a good time for you to help the child to associate the artist's name with these four examples of his or her work.

I suggested that you print the artist's name on the first set in each folder so that the child can notice it when she is looking at the four paintings by that artist. Even if a child cannot read, she will get a mental picture of the word representing the artist's name. The names are not printed on the other three sets because these four identical names would allow the child to use word clues rather than style clues to form the horizontal rows.

Children can become familiar with the names and works of many important artists in these *Step 3* exercises. Add more artists gradually, up to a maximum of six in each folder.

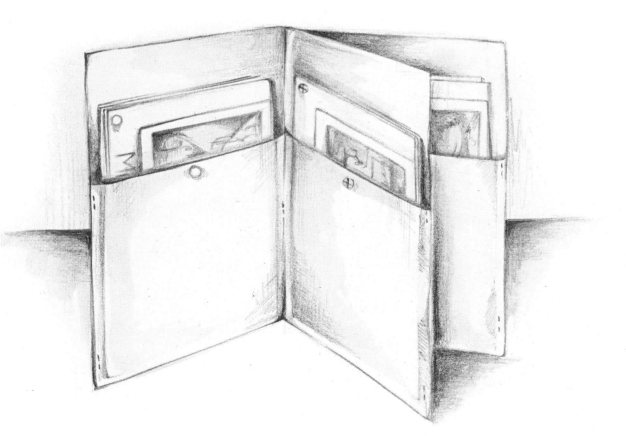

STEP 4 LEARNING THE NA[M]

Step 4 is designed for children who can read or are learning to read. It offers them the opportunity to become familiar with the names of many well-known artists by focusing on a particular subject, such as "Little Boys" or "Little Girls" and looking at examples of how six different artists treated this subject matter. The children can then learn the names of these six artists by referring to Control Cards and matching each artist's Name Card to his or her painting.

Selecting the Postcards

1. There are no separate Levels of difficulty for this *Step*. The challenge is approximately the same in each folder.

2. Because this *Step* is specifically designed for learning names, include only paintings by well-known artists, those whose names you will find consistently in art reference books or the Index of Artists on page 92.

3. The painting or paintings selected for each artist should be representative of the style for which he or she is most commonly known.

4. It is helpful to have some of the major artists represented in several different subject folders so that the children will begin to sense their importance and have repeated practice with their names. For example, paintings by Cezanne could be included under several of the following subjects: Flowers, Still Life, Landscapes, Women, Men, etc.

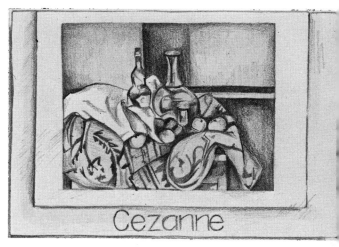

S OF THE ARTISTS

Materials

● At least three, but preferably six or more small yellow pocket-folders.

● Six 5" X 1" strips for each folder made from posterboard of the same color and weight as your mounting cards.

● Six duplicate pairs of mounted postcards for each folder. All six pairs feature the same subject matter, each pair by a different artist.

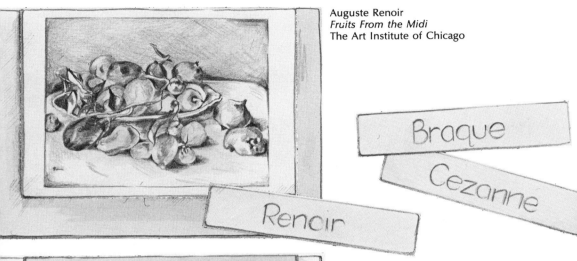

Auguste Renoir
Fruits From the Midi
The Art Institute of Chicago

Georges Braque
Still Life With Grapes
The Phillips Collection
Washington, D.C.

Preparing the Sets

1. On one mounting card of each identical pair in a folder, print the name of the artist in the space below the painting. All the cards in this first set are called "Control Cards."

2. Do not print the artists' names on the remaining mounted postcards which are called "Learning Cards."

3. Instead print an exact replica of each artist's name horizontally on a 5" X 1" strip. There will be six of these Name Cards for each folder.

4. Put the Control Cards in the left pocket of each folder.

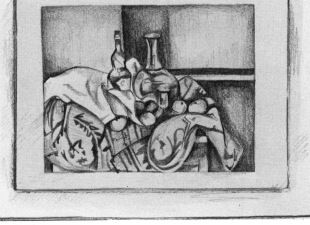

Paul Cezanne
Still Life with Peppermint Bottle
National Gallery of Art, Washington, D.C.

5. Put the Learning Cards and the Name Cards in the right pocket of the same folder. Spread out the Name Cards so they will not bulge in the pocket.

6. Paste an appropriate postcard on the cover and label each folder according to subject. For example: *Paintings of Children With Animals* or *Paintings of Mothers and Children.*

Note: Because the Control Cards are easily distinguished from the Learning Cards, no color-coding dots are necessary for this *Step.*

Demonstrating Step 4

1. Begin with a folder which contains paintings by some of the artists whose names you introduced in *Step 3.* Thus you can be sure that the child will not be immediately challenged by six "new" names.

2. Remove the Control Cards from the folder and place them in a vertical row saying each artist's name aloud as you handle his or her painting.

3. Explain to the child that the name below each painting is that of the artist who painted it.

4. Remove the Learning Cards from the folder and place each one beside its identical painting.

5. Remove the Name Cards from the folder and select the correct artist's name for each Learning Card by referring to the Control Card. Pronounce each artist's name again and place the Name Card below the painting.

6. When the layout is complete, point out to the child that each pair of paintings and names are identical.

7. Put the cards back in the folder and invite the child to do the exercise with the same folder. Ask her to pronounce the artists' names as she handles each Control Card and each Name Card.

Increasing the Difficulty

After a child has worked several times with a particular folder, show her how she can challenge herself by reversing the procedure:

1. Remove the materials from the right pocket and place the Learning Cards in a vertical row.

2. Place each artist's Name Card on the appropriate Learning Card while saying each name aloud.

3. Finally remove the Control Cards from the left pocket and place each painting beside its identical mate.

4. Check each Name Card with the Control Card beside it to be sure the names are identical.

5. Move the Name Cards *if* any corrections are necessary.

Follow the Child's Pace

When children are allowed to work in a relaxed atmosphere, they often achieve more than we expect. In my experience youngsters who cannot yet read fluently are sometimes able to do this exercise, apparently using the size and shape of the artist's name and its first letter as a guide. I have watched some of these children succeed; even those who cannot read short words like "does" or "play" can distinguish the name "Rembrandt" from the name "Van Gogh" and place each of these names in its appropriate place. Do not be concerned if a child does not immediately remember the artists' names. If you allow her to proceed at her own pace, she will commit them to memory gradually as she repeats the exercises over a period of weeks or months.

STEP 5 LEARNING THE NAME

It is neither necessary nor useful for young children to learn all the titles of the paintings which they experience in this project. Many titles such as *Composition 1* or *Untitled* are insignificant. Hundreds of paintings are called *Still Life* and hundreds of portraits are known by the names of the people who commissioned them—people who may or may not be noteworthy.

Many painters give the same name to several different compositions. Sometimes two or more painters use the same title, such as, *The Bridge at Chatou* which was painted by both Van Gogh and Vlaminck. Thus it would only be confusing for children to try to learn the titles of numerous paintings. It is, however, worthwhile for them to learn the names of a dozen or more very significant paintings which are widely known by their titles. Children can learn these in an exercise which is similar to *Step 4*.

Selecting the Paintings

There is no hard and fast list of famous paintings. Below is a selection of widely known works from which you can choose six for each folder. Don't hesitate to add others which you feel are significant.

Creation of Adam by Michelangelo
The Night Watch by Rembrandt
Mona Lisa by Leonardo
The Last Supper by Leonardo
Madonna of the Chair by Raphael
View of Toledo by El Greco
Birth of Venus by Botticelli
The Shrimp Girl by Hogarth
The Age of Innocence by Reynolds
Blue Boy by Gainsborough
Pinkie by Lawrence
Sunday Afternoon on the Island of La Grande Jatte by Seurat

The Swing by Fragonard
A Girl With A Watering Can by Renoir
The Starry Night by Van Gogh
The Lovers by Picasso
Peaceable Kingdom by Hicks
American Gothic by Grant Wood
George Washington by Gilbert Stuart
Arrangement in Black and Gray by Whistler
    (better known as *Whistler's Mother*)
Broadway Boogie-Woogie by Mondrian
Christina's World by Andrew Wyeth
Persistence of Memory by Salvador Dali

National Gallery of Art, Washington, D.C.

Tate Gallery, London

Materials

- Two to four tan pocket-folders.
- Twelve 5″ X ½″ strips of mounting card material for each folder.
- Six identical pairs of famous paintings for each folder.

Preparing the Sets and Folders

1. Make Control Cards by printing the name of the painting and the name of the artist (preceded by the word "by") on one mounting card of each identical pair in a folder. Since both names must fit in the space below the painting, use letters smaller than those which you used in *Step 4*.

2. Leave this space blank on the six Learning Cards.

3. On six of the posterboard strips, print the title of each of the paintings.

4. On the remaining six strips print the word "by" followed by the name of each of the artists.

5. Put the Control Cards in the left pocket of the folder.

6. Put the Learning Cards and all twelve strips in the right pocket of the folder.

7. Paste an appropriate art postcard on the cover of each folder; label them "Famous Paintings #1," "Famous Paintings #2" etc. Display.

Demonstrating Step 5

1. Begin with a folder containing at least some of the artists' names that the child learned in *Step 4*.

2. Proceed as in *Step 4* but now place a title as well as an artist's name on each Learning Card.

3. After considerable practice with each folder, encourage the child to match the Name Cards with the Learning Cards first and then use the Control Cards to check his work.

STEP 6 LEARNING ABOUT THE SCHOOLS OF ART

After a youngster can recognize the work of some of the major artists, he can begin to look at these artists as representatives of particular schools of art. A school of art is a group of artists whose paintings show a general similarity of style. They are often influenced by a particular region or country during a specific time period, such as the Seventeenth Century Dutch School. It is difficult for children, or even adults, to recognize the characteristics of the various schools of art when they are looking at random selections of paintings. However, when they concentrate on examples of the work of six artists from the same school, they are often able to detect the similarities of style. It is exciting to observe children recognizing these similarities. I once heard a six year-old remark, "They all look a little blurry," as he formed a row of paintings by six French Impressionist artists.

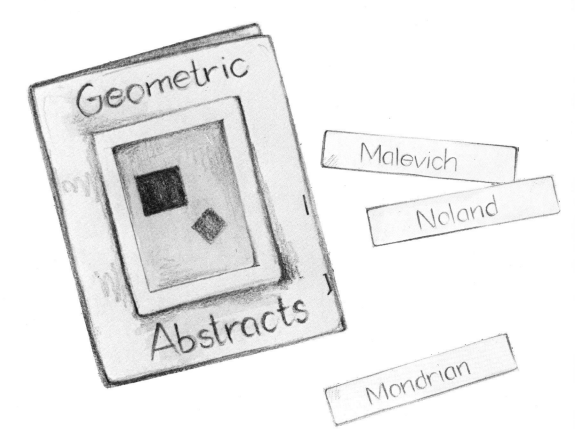

Kasimir Malevich
Suprematist Composition:
Red Square and
Black Square
Museum of Modern Art

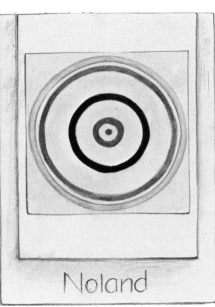

Kenneth Noland
Turnsole
Museum of Modern Art

Piet Mondrian
Broadway Boogie Woogie
Museum of Modern Art

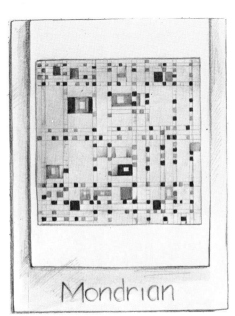

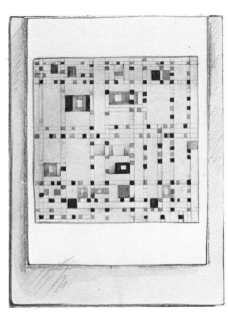

Materials

● At least six gray pocket-folders. This number can increase to about 24 depending on how far you want to expand your project.

● A 5″ X 1″ posterboard strip for each artist in each folder.

● Four to seven pairs of mounted identical paintings for each folder. Each pair is by a different artist, but all the paintings in each folder exhibit the characteristics of that particular school of art.

57

Selecting the Schools of Art for Step 6

1. Before preparing the folders for this *Step,* read the descriptions of the schools of art which begin on page 74.

2. Begin with about six selected schools of art. The choice can be arbitrary depending on what postcards you have available, but it is most effective if all six schools are very different from each other. I have found the following to be one good initial selection:

> Seventeenth Century Dutch Paintings
> French Impressionist Paintings
> Eighteenth Century British Portraits
> Geometric Abstract Paintings
> Primitive Paintings
> Japanese Paintings

3. As alternates or additions to the first group of schools use any of the other schools of art described in Part 3.

Note: Many of the names of the early Oriental and Primitive artists are not known. However, their paintings are so beautiful that they should be included in your Step 6 folders, even though it is not possible to associate an artist's name with every painting.

Preparing the Sets

Follow the instructions for *Step 4* except for labeling the cover. In *Step 6* label the cover of each folder according to the school of art. For example, *Cubist Paintings.*

Demonstrating Step 6

1. Begin with a folder containing some paintings which are familiar to the child.

2. Tell the child to do the exercise in the same way that he did those in *Step 4.*

3. When the cards are all laid out in rows, ask the child if he notices any similarities about all the paintings. Does he think they were painted recently or a long time ago? How do the people, houses, scenes, etc., look different from those of today?

4. Tell the child that all the paintings in that folder were done by artists who worked in a particular place and used a particular style. Therefore we say that they belong to a particular school of art.

5. Point to the name of the school on the cover of the folder and find the location of that school on a world map.

Other Uses for These Step 6 Folders

It is worthwhile to make a considerable number of folders for *Step 6* because you will use them again for *Step 7* and *Step 8*. In addition, these school of art folders are appropriate to use in a history, geography or cultural unit whenever children are studying a particular portion of history or a particular country of the world. For example, Early American paintings can be coor-

dinated with a study of colonial or eighteenth century American history. Italian masters will be perfect illustrations for studying the Renaissance. And Oriental paintings are excellent visual aids for a study of China or Japan. You will find these school of art folders a delightful addition to any home or classroom environment.

STEP 7 GROUPING PAINTINGS FROM THE SAME SCHOOL OF ART

This is a sorting exercise to give children practice in distinguishing one school of art from another. The Control Cards from the folders of three schools of art are mixed together and the child sorts them by placing the cards from each school in a horizontal row.

Selecting Schools of Art

LEVEL 1

The easiest combinations are three schools which are very different from each other, e.g. British, Geometric Abstract and Japanese.

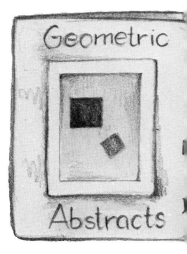

LEVEL 2

A more challenging combination is two schools which have some similarities and a contrasting one, e.g. American Impressionists, American Realists and Spanish.

LEVEL 3

The most challenging combination is three schools which are somewhat similar to each other, e.g. Flemish, Italian and Dutch.

Lawrence

Gainsborough

Materials

● A triple black sorting folder (see page 72).

● At least three but preferably nine, *Step 6* folders, complete with mounted cards, for each level.

Mondrian

Noland

Increasing the Challenge by Rearranging

If you have folders for nine schools of art, you can probably use these for all three levels, simply by rearranging them. Many different combinations are possible. Following is just one example of how rearranging can increase the challenge at each Level:

Start with the easiest combinations for Level 1—

British Geometric Abstract Japanese

French Abstract Post-Impressionist

Dutch Cubist Impressionist

Rearrange these for a little more challenge for Level 2—

British Dutch Impressionist

French Geometric Abstract Cubist

Abstract Post-Impressionist Japanese

Preparing the Exercise for Step 7

Make a triple sorting folder according to the instructions on page 71. Stock this triple folder in the following way:

1. Select three school of art folders appropriate for the child's level.

2. Remove the six Control Cards from the first of these school of art folders, and place one of them in each of the six pockets in the black folder.

3. Do the same with the Control Cards from the second and third school of art folders.

4. You will now have three Control Cards in each of the six pockets of the black folder. Mix up the consecutive order of the cards in each pocket.

Rearrange again for
the greatest challenge
for Level 3—

British
French
Dutch

Geometric Abstract
Abstract
Cubist

Impressionist
Post-Impressionist
Japanese

Demonstrating Step 7

The object of the exercise is to arrange the paintings from the black folder in three horizontal rows, each headed by a gray folder identifying a school of art and beside it, paintings by six different artists from that school.

1. Place the three gray folders from which you have removed the Control Cards in a vertical row.

2. Remove the three paintings from the first pocket of the black folder, and place each one beside the school of art folder to which it belongs.

3. Continue this procedure, using the cards from all six pockets, one pocket at a time.

Correcting Errors

One of the advantages of this exercise is that the person doing the exercise—teacher or child—can correct it herself:

1. Remove the Learning Cards from the right-hand pocket of the first gray folder.

2. Lay each Learning Card on top of its identical Control Card in the first horizontal row.

3. If you have any Learning Card that does not match a Control Card in the first row, you know an error has been made and should be corrected.

4. Continue checking each row by the same procedure.

5. For further practice with names of the artists,

match the Name Cards in each gray folder to the Control Cards in each row, saying the artist's name aloud as you do so.

6. After completing the exercise, place the Control Cards from each horizontal row in the left-hand pocket of the gray folder to which they belong.

7. Place the Learning Cards and Name Cards from each row in the right-hand pocket of the appropriate folder. The black folder is now empty, ready to be used again.

8. Stock the black folder again and invite a child to do the exercise.

Expanding the Exercise

Add several more schools of art to the black folder, one school at a time. The child can then sort four, five and eventually six schools of art in this exercise.

A child will be able to do this advanced work only after a great deal of practice with the various

schools of art. Never insist that a child memorize the names of the artists in a particular school of art. Let him come to know these artists gradually and naturally through frequent repetition of the exercises in *Step 6* and *Step 7*.

STEP 8 USING A TIME LIN

After a child has become familiar with a number of the important artists and schools of art, he can begin to locate them in history by placing art folders or postcard paintings beside a Time Line. Essentially a Time Line is a long strip of paper or plastic about 10 to 15 inches wide on which a series of dates is printed at specific intervals. It is a very useful device for graphically illustrating art history or any other kind of history because it gives children a visual representation of consecutive events. To use a Time Line, a child must know how to read dates and understand their meaning.

Before making any of the Time Lines described below read the detailed instructions on page 73. The length of any Time Line, as well as the span of its intervals, is determined by the subject and the period of history which it illustrates. For example, if you were making a Time Line of the Presidents of the United States, you would begin with 1789 and continue the dates at four-year intervals up to the present time. If you allowed four inches for every four-year interval, the Time Line would be about 17 feet long. A child working with this Time Line would stretch it out on the floor and put each president's picture and name beside the date when he took office.

Making Three Basic Time Lines

Time Lines of art history are not so evenly calibrated or as well defined. In my experience I have found that history of art can be best illustrated by three basic Time Lines, representing three consecutive periods of art history. Each of these Time Lines is calibrated differently to accommodate the volume of paintings from that portion of history.

1. Ancient and Medieval—This Time Line begins in 3000 B.C. and continues until 1300 A.D.—a period of 4300 years. Art that has survived from the early years of recorded history is dated by century rather than a specific year. Therefore five hundred year intervals are adequate for this early segment of history. Divide your Time Line into eleven equal segments. With a thick black marker print the title—*Ancient and Medieval Art*—in the first segment. Use a thick red marker to print the date 3000 B.C. in the second segment. Continue printing the following dates in red: 2500 B.C., 2000 B.C., 1500 B.C., 1000 B.C., 500 B.C.

Print the remaining dates in the A.D. period with a black marker: 1 A.D., 500 A.D., 1000 A.D., 1300 A.D.

2. Traditional Art—This Time Line begins with the Renaissance in 1300 and continues through 1850. Fifty-year intervals are used to accommodate the painting of this prolific period of 550 years. Divide your Time Line into thirteen equal segments. With a black marker print the title in the first segment and the following dates in the remaining segments: 1300, 1350, 1400, 1450, 1500, 1550, 1600, 1650, 1700, 1750, 1800, 1850.

3. Modern Art—This Time Line begins with the Impressionists in 1850 and continues to the present time. Since so many rapidly changing styles of Modern Art belong in this period, it is best displayed in ten year intervals. With a black marker print the title in the first segment and the year 1850 in the second segment. Continue with every tenth year: 1860, 1870, 1880, etc., up to the present time.

OF ART

Some Special Time Lines

1. A Child's Own Time Line—A delightful way to introduce a child to history as the story of consecutive events is to help him to make a Time Line of his own life with one segment for each year. This Time Line begins with the year of his birth beside which he can place the earliest photograph of himself—also pictures of his parents or other important people in his life during that year. Beside the second date, one year later, place his picture taken around the time of his first birthday. Continue these pictures to the present time including photographs of new brothers and sisters, new pet, new house, starting to school, vacations, etc. The child's mounted photographs may be kept in an orange folder with his picture on the cover and labeled with his name, e.g. "Michael's Time Line."

2. A Time Line of Pre-historic Painting—If the children with whom you work are interested in the Cave Paintings and you wish to dramatize how very old these paintings are, you can make a Pre-historic Time Line beginning with the year 20,000 B.C. and continuing until 3000 B.C. Use 1000 year intervals and print all dates in red. Place postcards of the cave paintings beside the first few dates—20,000 B.C., 19,000 B.C., 18,000 B.C.— and then no more postcards until the Egyptian tomb paintings in 3000 B.C. This Time Line graphically portrays the long intervening period from which we presently have very few surviving examples of painting.

3. A sequence of paintings by one particular artist—Five-year intervals should be used for an individual artist, beginning with the date of his or her earliest work. Picasso is the most obvious choice for an individual Time Line because he made many significant style changes during his long lifetime. In fact, a Time Line display is one of the most dramatic ways of looking at Picasso's work. Other artists whose paintings make interesting Time Lines are Matisse, Goya, Chagall and Monet.

Using Your School of Art Folders with the Basic Time Lines

For a child's initial Time Line exercise select one of the three basic Time Lines which will accommodate some of the folders of the schools of art which you prepared for *Step 6.* Show the child how to place each folder beside the Time Line near the date when that school was active. Later he can use all three Time Lines in sequence to accommodate all the folders which you have made. If you have a complete set beginning with the Egyptian tomb paintings and continuing through modern abstracts, the cover paintings on these folders will form a beautiful display of the consecutive major developments in art history. Even if you have only a few of the school of art folders, it is worthwhile placing them on the Time Lines to give the child an idea of the sequential relationship of these schools to each other.

Later the child can use these same materials to make a much more elaborate display. He can remove the Control Cards from each folder and place them beside their appropriate dates in a horizontal row perpendicular to the Time Line. This impressive display will then feature about six examples from each school.

New Sequences for Your Basic Time Lines

Actually your Step 6 materials are only the first of many delightful sequences that can be displayed on your Time Lines. Next I suggest you make orange folders containing postcards selected specifically to illustrate interesting developments in painting.

1. A sequence of paintings of a particular subject by artists from many countries over a lengthy period of time:

When one subject, such as "Mother and Child," is displayed on a Time Line, it is easy for a child to observe changes in the way this subject was painted through several centuries—differences in dress, differences in formality or informality, in backgrounds, in style, etc. These changes are noticeable only if every painting has the same subject matter. They are not nearly so evident if you use a random selection of subjects.

Any of the following are good subjects for a Time Line because each of them was painted by a great number of the important artists in history: Men, Women, Children, Landscapes, Still Life, Mothers and Children and Musicians.

The subject of Musicians—not paintings of composers but paintings of persons playing musical instruments—is particularly interesting. Because a Time Line of Musicians shows the very old instruments such as lutes and harpsichords, it is fun to coordinate this Time Line with listening to some of the music written for these instruments during a particular time in history.

2. A sequence of paintings from a particular country, such as "Spanish Painting from El Greco to Dali" or "American Painting from Colonial Times to the Present":

This sequence can be used for many different countries, especially Italy, France, Germany, England, China and Japan. It is particularly effective for illustrating the many changes in the style of American art in a relatively short period of history. See pages 87-90. Both of the sequences described above can be used with your three basic Time Lines.

Preparing Folders for New Sequences

When preparing postcards for your orange pocket-folders, print the name of the artist and the date of the painting on the front of each mounting card. This date is usually found on the reverse side of the postcard. If the date of the painting is not included with the information there, use the dates of the artist's life and put them in parentheses. When placing the card beside the Time Line, assume that the date of the painting would be some time after the mid-point of the artist's life.

Prepare your double orange folder according to the directions on page 71. Not all sequences will have exactly 24 paintings. To determine the number of folders to be stapled together for one sequence allow one folder for each 12 postcards. Mix up the sequential order of the dates before storing the mounted cards in the pockets. Place a directly related art postcard on the cover and label each folder according to its subject. For example, *Time Line of Men* or *Time Line of American Art*.

Demonstrating the Time Line

It is fun to do a Time Line with two, three or four youngsters:

1. Let the children help you to unroll or unfold the Time Line carefully.

2. Explain that the Time Line will enable them to see the consecutive order of paintings and/or schools of art from a long time ago up to more recent times.

3. Have the children read some of the dates and explain the number of years represented by the space between each date.

4. Remove a mounted card from an orange folder. Read its date aloud and then place it beside the Time Line within the appropriate time span.

5. Do the same with several more cards and then give each child a card to place beside the Time Line.

6. Divide the remaining cards among the children and let them finish the Time Line, making sure they read each date aloud.

7. Whenever several cards belong in the same time span, place them in a horizontal row, perpendicular to the Time Line. If your collection of postcards is a balanced representation of each important school of art, these rows will graphically illustrate periods of high productivity. Conversely, there will be no cards or only a few cards for years of low productivity or periods from which very few examples have survived.

8. If possible, let the finished Time Line remain in place for several hours, or even several days, so the children can absorb the details and talk about them.

9. When you are ready to put the Time Line away, show the children how to mix up the order of the cards and replace them in the pockets of the orange folder. Then let the youngsters help you to roll or fold the Time Line carefully for storage.

PART THREE

CONVENIENT
REFERENCES

SHOPPING LIST

All the basic materials except the art postcards are available at stationary or office supply stores.

For use in Step:	8½x11 or 9x12 pocket folders	22"x28" sheets of medium posterboard	Art Postcards*
1	3 red	3	18 identical pairs
2	3 blue	3	18 companion pairs
3	6 green	3	4 by each of 9 artists
4	3 yellow	3	6 identical pairs for each of 3 subjects
5	2 tan	2	12 identical pairs of famous paintings
6	6 gray	5	6 identical pairs for each of 6 schools of art
7	3 black		
8	2 orange	2	24 on one subject

¼" color-coding dots: 1 pkg. each, yellow, green, red, black

*Pre-arranged sets of art postcards that can be used with all the Steps in this manual have been prepared by the author. For ordering information send a self-addressed stamped envelope to **PARENT CHILD PRESS**
P.O. Box 767
Altoona, PA 16603

HOW TO MOUNT YOUR POSTCARDS

Material:

Medium-weight posterboard.

Color:

White, off-white, light gray or light beige. Select any one of these colors and use it throughout your entire project.

Size:

5" X 7"

Sixteen 5" X 7" cards can be cut from a standard 22" X 28" sheet. Use a large paper-cutter, if available.

Placement:

1. Put the top edge of the postcard at the top edge of the mounting card, leaving one inch below the postcard for printing an identifying name whenever necessary.

2. Center each postcard left to right.

Mounting Choices:

Hinge or hinges—Access to information on the reverse side of the postcards can be maintained if the postcard is hinged to the mounting card. Use library tape or adhesive tape to make three hinges—each a total of two inches in length— for each card. Attach these hinges to the reverse side of the postcard and the front of the mounting card as shown. These small tape hinges, however, sometimes break from frequent use. One large hinge—about 3" X 3"—made from laminate or clear adhesive paper is much longer lasting.

Pasting—Use a good quality paste to attach the postcard permanently to the mounting card. Before pasting, copy the identifying information from the reverse side of the postcard and print it on the back of the mounting card, or photo-copy the reverse side of the postcard and paste the photo copy on the back of the mounting card.

Laminating—Although laminating is the most expensive method of mounting, it is also the most durable and is recommended for postcards that will be heavily used. Before laminating, put the identifying information on the back of the mounting card. Also put any necessary identifying symbol or name on the mounting card before covering both the mounting card and postcard with laminate.

Note: Clear adhesive paper, also called clear contact paper, is *not* recommended for covering the postcards because it darkens the colors in the paintings.

HOW TO MAKE SMALL POCKET FOLDERS

Buy 8" X 11" or 9" X 12" pocket-folders in the color designated for the *Step* you are preparing and cut them to the 6" X 8" size:

1. With the folder closed, measure to a point 8" above the bottom edge and 6" from the left or folded edge.

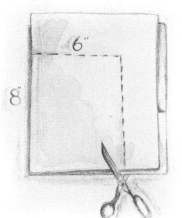

2. From this point draw a 6" horizontal line to the folded edge and an 8" vertical line to the bottom edge.

3. Cut the closed folder on these lines.

4. Use staples or glue to close the outside edge of each pocket where it was cut off.

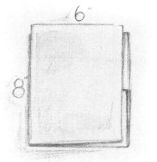

5. When making a double folder for *Step 3* or *Step 8* attach the back cover of one folder to the front cover of a second folder with either paste, rubber cement or staples.

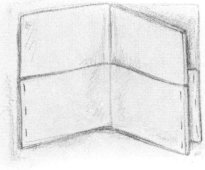

THE SORTING FOLDER FOR STEP 7

Because there are usually eighteen different paintings in three school of art folders, you will need a large (9″ X 12″ or 8½″ X 11″) sorting folder with six pockets. Make the triple folder in this way:

1. Attach the back cover of one black pocket-folder to the front cover of a second black pocket-folder with a row of staples along the front edge.

2. Attach the back cover of this double folder to the front cover of a third black folder by the same means.

3. Paste several art postcards on the cover and label it "Sorting Folder."

4. Leave the pockets empty when it is not in use and store the sorting folder near your *Step Six* folders.

A SAMPLE OF MANUSCRIPT LETTERING

The manuscript lettering illustrated below is a good clear style to use when you are printing on mounting cards or folders.

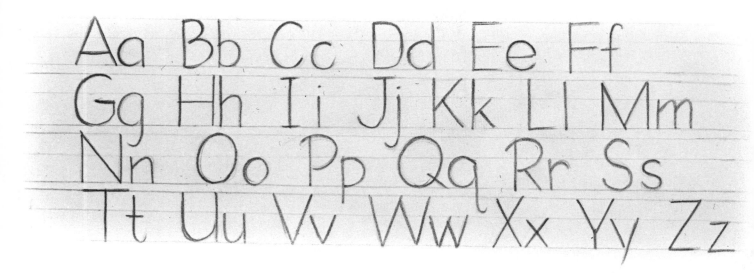

HOW TO MAKE TIME LINES

Here are two different methods for making Time Lines:

1. Use unlined computer paper which folds accordian-style on perforated creases. Print one date on each sheet. This Time Line has the advantage of lying flat on the floor and folding easily for storage. However, unless it is handled carefully, it may tear on the perforated folds.

2. For a more durable Time Line, use white plastic shelf paper that is about 12" wide. If you cannot obtain a roll of this paper long enough for the Time Line you wish to make, sew or staple several pieces together, end to end, to form the length you desire. Use horizontal lines about 12" apart to divide this Time Line into equal segments, and print one date in each segment. Then use staples or strong tape to attach each end to a wooden dowel. The dowels help to hold the Time Line flat on the floor when it is in use. Roll the Time Line around one of the dowels for easy storage.

A Time Line which can be used on the floor.

Where to Place Time Lines

Children are most comfortable using a Time Line on the floor because it is very easy for them to place any number of art postcards beside it. However, a Time Line project on the floor takes a great deal of space, and it is often not practical to leave it on display for more than a few hours or a few days.

A Time Line on the wall can usually remain in place for longer periods. It should be mounted horizontally at a height which is convenient for the children who will use it. If you hang the Time Line directly above a chalk tray or above a long low shelf, the children can stand the postcards on the chalk tray or shelf and lean them against their appropriate dates on the Time Line. If you have no chalk tray or long shelf available, then mount the Time Line on the wall at floor level and the children can lay the postcards on the floor in front of it.

A Time Line which can be mounted horizontally on the wall or used on the floor.

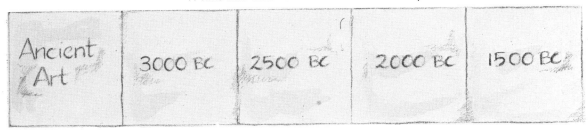

THE SCHOOLS OF ART IN HISTORY

Altar Piece
King Balthasar
Barcelona
12th Century

The following summaries of some of the important schools in art history are for your own quick reference when you are preparing the postcard activities, presenting them to children and answering their questions.

Because this entire project is designed for children, I have simplified these descriptions as much as possible. In no way are they intended to be complete or definitive. The history of art is long and complicated. A detailed knowledge is helpful but certainly not essential for working with art postcards.

A school of art is a group of artists whose paintings show a general similarity of style because they shared a particular influence during a specific time period. Because classifying the work of painters is not an exact science, many art reference books differ in the way they delineate the schools of art and the selection of artists that are included. The style of some painters is so individual that they cannot be classified in any of the commonly recognized schools, and the style of others, particularly modern artists, is so varied that they are included in two or three different schools.

It is important to understand that the making of art is a continuous process with artists borrowing techniques or taking inspiration from what has gone before them. Some artists build on the work of those who immediately preceded them while others reach back through the centuries for their models. Thus many modern painters owe more to primitive art than to the formalities of later European painting.

For convenience, I have divided the history of art into three segments which will correspond to the three basic Time Lines mentioned in earlier sections of this text. These divisions are Ancient and Medieval Art from 3000 B.C. to 1300 A.D. Traditional Art from 1300 to 1850 and Modern Art from 1850 to the present. Preceding these three divisions of recorded history are the Cave Paintings.

PREHISTORIC ART

The Cave Paintings

The earliest known paintings are the Cave Paintings which date back to about 20,000 B.C. They were discovered during the past one hundred years on the walls of caves in France and Spain. The Cave Paintings have a simple flat appearance and each one usually features a single animal. Sometimes this animal is one which no longer exists or else lives only in regions much further north. The artists used paints made from clay and stones, limiting the colors to the earth tones.

These pre-historic paintings have survived because they were preserved in the darkness and special atmospheric conditions which exist deep within caves or tombs. Very few examples of painting have been discovered from the long period of approximately 14,000 years which followed the Cave Paintings.

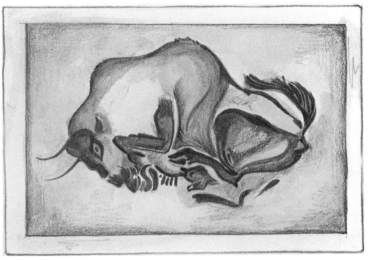

Paleolithic painting
Female Bison
Cave of Altamira

ANCIENT AND MEDIEVAL ART

Although much more detailed and elaborate than the Cave Paintings, the paintings from 3000 B.C. to 1300 A.D. were limited to the same two-dimensional appearance because the technique of perspective and the use of shadows had not yet been adequately developed.

Egyptian Paintings

Recorded history began in Egypt about 3000 B.C. Much of it was revealed to us through the discovery of elaborate tombs which had been prepared for kings and noblemen. The walls of the rooms inside the tombs were covered with paintings of everyday life—hunting, fishing, harvesting, eating, playing music, dancing, making jewelry, cutting hair, attending a party and many other activities. Most of the faces are shown in profile with the shoulders facing front, indicating that these artists had difficulty drawing a full face or a side view of the shoulder. Most of the women in the paintings are wearing strange black wigs and their skin is painted a much lighter color than that of the men. Indeed most of the women look alike and most of the men look alike, since the artists made no attempt to portray any individual characteristics.

Egyptian tomb painting
Guests and Musicians
18th Dynasty

Paintings from Crete

The Palace of Minos was discovered in recent years on the island of Crete. Paintings on its walls portray animals, flowers, birds and imaginary scenes, as well as human figures. Here the men are also painted with skin darker than the women, but both men and women are freer and more graceful than in the Egyptian paintings. This art dates from 2000 B.C. to 1200 A.D. Other wall paintings depicting scenes of hunts and battles have been discovered in the Palace of Mycenae and the Palace of Tiryns.

Greek, Etruscan and Roman Painting

From the seventh to the third century B.C. the Greeks produced their finest thinkers and artists. Because many famous examples of sculpture and architecture from this period still survive, we tend to speak of the masterpieces of Greek art as temples and statues. Painting, however, was equally important at the time. Unfortunately, all the paintings which decorated the walls of the temples have been destroyed. The only remaining examples of Greek painting from this famous period are the beautiful "vase paintings" with which they decorated their pottery.

Some experts believe that the lost paintings of the Greeks may have resembled the Etruscan tomb paintings which date from the fifth century B.C. The Etruscans, who lived in what is now central Italy, were great admirers of the Greeks. The figures in their paintings are well proportioned and have an almost three dimensional appearance.

Both the Greeks and the Etruscans influenced the art of the Romans who conquered them. Many of the Roman wall paintings from the first century B.C. and the first century A.D. survive because of a catastrophe—they were buried, and thus preserved, by the eruption of Vesuvius in 79 A.D. These paintings located in Pompeii, Herculaneum and Stabiae include landscapes, portraits, still lifes and garden scenes. Some have an airy quality that is almost impressionistic.

The tomb paintings in the city of Rome which date from the early centuries A.D. are known as the Catacomb Paintings and are the first paintings to exhibit Christian themes.

Painting in the Middle Ages

During the Middle Ages the monasteries and the churches kept the arts alive in Europe when most of that continent was engulfed in wars, plagues and poverty. From the 5th century A.D. to about the 15th century A.D., Western Art was almost entirely influenced by the early Christian Church which used paintings as a means of teaching the Gospels. These paintings were often done on wet plaster in churches or on wooden altar pieces. When done on wet plaster, they were called *frescoes*. Illustrations of gospel stories also took the form of *illuminated manuscripts* painted by monks. The most famous of the illuminated manuscripts is the *Book of Kells* from the 8th century which contains some of the most intricate designs ever made and is decorated with gold leaf. The figures, however, like those in the Egyptian paintings have no body contours or depth.

Book of Kells
The Virgin and Child
Late 8th Century

TRADITIONAL EUROPEAN ART

What is frequently referred to as "Traditional Art" began with the use of perspective in the 14th century and extended to the beginning of Modern Art in 1850. The early centuries of Traditional Art continued to serve the work of the Christian Church so that religious themes predominated.

Italian Renaissance

Near the end of the 14th century a great change came about in Europe, a change which has been called *Renaissance* meaning re-birth. Inspired by a growth in trade, travel, nationalism and learning, this period, which is known for its rich development in culture and art, began in Florence, Italy. Here master artists taught young apprentices to mix paint for frescoes and tempera—a sort of water color thickened with egg yolks—which was used to paint altar pieces on wooden boards. Oil paint was not in use during the early Renaissance.

The earliest artist to make human figures life-like was Giotto, who actually preceded the Renaissance by one hundred years. His figures were not perfect but they were rounded rather than flat, and they had human expressions on their faces. Giotto's backgrounds, however, had no real depth.

For the next two centuries one great artist followed another. These great Italian Renaissance painters studied anatomy so thoroughly that they were able to portray the human body perfectly in any position. They also mastered the techniques of perspective enabling them to depict objects at any distance from the eye of the viewer. Three of the greatest artists of the Italian Renaissance were Leonardo da Vinci, who was renowned for his accurate scientific drawings as well as his paintings; Raphael, who was known for the beauty of his composition and figures; and Michaelangelo, who executed the monumental paintings on the ceiling of the Sistine Chapel in Rome.

Michelangelo
Head of Etruscan Sibyl
Sistine Chapel, Rome

Italian Renaissance Painters
Early Renaissance—14th-15th centuries
Giotto di Bondone 1266-1337
Fra Angelico 1387-1455
Fra Filippo Lippi 1406-1469
Pierro della Francesco 1416-1492
Sandro Botticelli 1444-1510

High Renaissance—16th century
Leonardo da Vinci 1452-1519
Michelangelo Buonarroti 1475-1564
Titian (Tiziano Vecellio) 1477-1576
Antonio Allegri Correggio 1495-1534
Raphael Sanzio 1483-1520
Jacopo Tintoretto 1518-1594

Northern Renaissance Painting

At the time of the Italian Renaissance, another group of outstanding painters were working in Flanders (now Belgium) and Germany. Their work is often referred to as Northern Renaissance painting.

The earliest of the great Flemish painters was Jan van Eyck, whose painting *The Annunciation* is a marvel of perspective. He was the first to mix powdered color with an oil base rather than an egg base, thus inventing the slow-drying oil paint used by all great masters who followed him. Unlike the formerly used tempera which had dried so quickly, the oil paint could be blended on the canvas. While the Renaissance painters of Italy made a special study of the anatomy of the body and the portrayal of movement, the painters of the North specialized in studying the surface of everything they painted—its texture, color and the effect of light on it—and they carefully put every tiny detail on their canvases. Rubens is particularly noted for his beautiful skin textures and the Bruegels for their detailed scenes with many people.

The great German painter, Dürer, who was also a scientist and an engraver, is renowned for exact details such as fur of animals and perfectly drawn muscles. The two Holbeins were famous for the extraordinary beauty of their portraits.

German Painters

Albrecht Dürer 1471-1528
Hans Holbein, the Younger 1497-1543
Lukas Cranach, the Elder 1472-1553
Ambrosius Holbein 1494-1520
Albrecht Altdorfer 1480-1538

Flemish Painters

Peter Paul Rubens 1577-1640
Jacob Jordaens 1593-1678
Rogier van der Weyden 1400-1464
Hans Memling 1435-1494
Hieronymus Bosch 1450-1516
Pieter Bruegel the Elder 1525-1569
Jan Brueghel 1568-1625
Jan van Eyck 1385-1441
Anthony van Dyck 1599-1641
Jan Gossaert 1478-1533

Spanish Painting from 16th to 18th Century

Spain's first great painter, known as El Greco, was actually a Greek who lived in Spain during the 16th century. El Greco's paintings can be recognized by their distortion. He deliberately elongated and twisted his human figures to make them more dramatic. In the next generation the greatest painter was Velasquez who served as the artist for the king's court and was known for the perfect likenesses of his portraits. He was followed by Murillo whose work included religious scenes on very large canvases and street scenes showing urchins eating and playing games. One hundred years after Velasquez, the Spanish court had another great artist—Goya—whose portraits did not flatter his subjects but mocked them in caricature. He also painted scenes of daily life and was noted for his etchings of beasts and monsters.

Velazquez
Don Baltasar Carlos
The Wallace Collection
London

Spanish Painters

El Greco 1541-1614   Diego Velásquez 1599-1660
Jusepe da Ribera 1590-1652   Bartolomé Murillo 1617-1682
Francisco Zurbarán 1598-1664   Francisco de Goya 1748-1828

Seventeenth Century Dutch Painting

Instead of religious themes, the 17th century Dutch painters portrayed the new middle-class society in portraiture and scenes from daily life. DeHooch painted warm family scenes (which often included a geometric pattern of floor tiles) and Vermeer featured portraits of women quietly working. The roisterous life of the tavern was portrayed by Hals and Metsu. Both Rembrandt and Ruisdael created spectacular lighting in their landscapes. Rembrandt, of course, surpassed all the other artists with his profound portraiture. While other 17th century artists painted man's outward appearance, Rembrandt was concerned with the depth of the human soul, revealing both its grandeur and its misery in dramatic encounters of light and dark. It is remarkable that so many great artists lived and worked in the tiny country of Holland during this short period of time.

Dutch Painters

Frans Hals 1580-1666   Jacob van Ruisdael 1628-1682
Rembrandt van Rijn 1606-1669   Gabriel Metsu 1629-1667
Gerard Ter Borch 1617-1681   Pieter de Hooch 1629-1688
Aelbert Cuyp 1620-1691   Johannes Vermeer 1632-1675
Jan Steen 1626-1679   Judith Leyster 1610-1660
                                 Meindert Hobbema 1638-1709

Johannes Vermeer
The Kitchen-maid
Rijksmuseum, Amsterdam

18th Century French Painting

French painters in the 18th century often depicted the carefree life of courtiers—beautiful maidens and handsome youths amusing themselves. This art can be characterized as idyllic, portraying life romantically rather than realistically. Because the French preferred delicate, soft lines and pastel colors, these 18th century paintings have sometimes been criticized as being more *pretty* than beautiful. The greatest painter of palace life was Watteau, who often portrayed travelling companies of actors. In the next generation Boucher was noted for his portraits of ladies of the court and Fragonard for his graceful figures in landscapes with soaring trees and puffy white clouds. Chardin, on the other hand, painted the simple home life of the people.

Fragonard *The Swing*
The Wallace Collection, London

French Painters

Antoine Watteau 1684-1721
Jean Baptiste Chardin 1699-1779
François Boucher 1703-1770
Jean Baptiste Perroneau 1715-1783
Jean Baptiste Greuze 1725-1805
François Drouais 1727-1775
Jean-Honoré Fragonard 1732-1806

18th Century British Painting

Until the 18th century, the British felt that all good art must come from abroad. Hogarth was the first English artist to prove that an Englishman could paint as well as a foreigner. Hogarth's subjects were the common people and his portrayal of them in their everyday work was a social comment on his times.

The work of the portrait artists who followed Hogarth had a much different look. These artists—Reynolds, Gainsborough, Romney and Lawrence—painted the wealthy people who commissioned portraits for their homes. In these portraits the subjects were usually dressed lavishly but their costumes were not always indicative of the style of that time. Many of their portraits of children have become favorites around the world.

British Painters

William Hogarth 1697-1764
Joshua Reynolds 1723-1792
Thomas Gainsborough 1727-1788
George Romney 1734-1802
Henry Raeburn 1756-1823
Thomas Lawrence 1769-1830

Joshua Reynolds
The Age of Innocence
Tate Gallery, London

Nineteenth Century Romanticism, Realism and Neoclassicism

In the first half of the nineteenth century a new spirit of non-conformity and artistic freedom influenced the work of European painters. Known as Romanticism, this movement covered a wide range of subjects—landscapes, seascapes, portraits, drama, mythological scenes and mystical works. Each of the Romantic painters had a very individual style. Constable's landscapes and Turner's seascapes subdue concrete details with the drama of wind, sunlight and clouds. Blake, who was obsessed with Milton, Dante and the Bible, created mystical drawings which were highly symbolic. The movement flourished in both England and France, but perhaps the greatest of all Romantic painters was Francisco de Goya of Spain.

With the new scientific developments of the second half of the nineteenth century, Romanticism declined in popularity. Three Frenchmen—Courbet, Daumier and Millet—were the greatest of the new Realists who portrayed everyday life with frankness and authenticity.

Neoclassicism was a less important movement that abandoned elaborate detail in favor of the clean style of ancient Roman and Greek sculpture.

Francisco de Goya
Grape-gathering

Romantic Painters

Francisco de Goya 1748-1828
William Blake 1757-1827
J.M.W. Turner 1775-1851
John Constable 1776-1837
Camille Corot 1796-1875
Eugene Delacroix 1798-1863
Theodore Géricault 1791-1824
Theodore Rousseau 1821-1867

Realist Painters

Gustave Courbet 1819-1877
François Millet 1814-1875
Honoré Daumier 1808-1879

Neoclassicist Painters

Jacques Louis David 1748-1825
Antoine Gros 1771-1835
Jean-Auguste Ingres 1780-1867

MODERN ART

In the mid 19th century a new era of art began which led step by step from the realistic representations of traditional art through a variety of contemporary schools and arrived ultimately at completely abstract art in which no real persons or objects can be identified.

Impressionism

Impressionism is the great turning point from traditional painting to modern art. It began in France about 1860 and flourished there for about twenty years. The Impressionist painters turned away from the strict representation of reality and produced instead a somewhat blurry image or an "impression" of a subject. To do this they abandoned the careful preparation which had been customary in the indoor studios and moved their canvases outdoors where they could spontaneously paint their perceptions of nature. For example, when painting a garden they no longer neatly outlined every flower, leaf and stem. Instead they painted what they actually saw— bright splashes of color. They were also fascinated with the ever changing outdoor light and sometimes made several paintings of the same scene, each at a different time of day. By subduing the details of their subject matter, the Impressionists paved the way for the more abstract art of the 20th Century.

Post-Impressionism

Post-Impressionism is not one particular style but a name for several different styles, all of which developed as reactions against Impressionism. The artists were French or worked in France from about 1880 to about 1910. Because they felt that Impressionism was too limiting, the Post-Impressionists innovated in several different

Auguste Renoir *A Girl With A Watering Can*
National Gallery of Art, Washington, D.C.

French Impressionist Painters

Camille Pissarro 1830-1903
Edgar Degas 1834-1917
Claude Monet 1840-1926
Berthe Morisot 1841-1895
Edouard Manet 1832-1883
Alfred Sisley 1839-1899
Pierre Auguste Renoir 1841-1919

Van Gogh
The Starry Night
Museum of Modern Art
New York

ways. Georges Seurat and Paul Signac used *pointillism,* that is painting with separate dots of pure color so that the mixing of colors takes place in the eye of the viewer. Toulouse-Lautrec's cabaret scenes were tinged with caricature. Deep emotion characterized the paintings of both Van Gogh, who used thick, surging, twisting strokes, and Gauguin, who used broad, simple flat tones. One of the most important Post-Impressionists, Cezanne, stressed the geometric structures that make up many scenes in nature and thereby began to formalize the casual character of Impressionism. His emphasis on these geometric patterns led the way to Cubism.

Paul Gauguin
Crouching Tahitian Girl
Art Institute of Chicago

Post-Impressionist Painters

Paul Cezanne 1839-1906
Georges Seurat 1859-1891
Paul Signac 1863-1935
Edouard Vuillard 1868-1940

Gustave Moreau 1826-1898
Maurice Utrillo 1883-1955
Vincent Van Gogh 1853-1890
Henri de Toulouse-Lautrec 1864-1901

Paul Gauguin 1848-1903
Pierre Bonnard 1867-1947
Odilon Redon 1840-1916

Fauvism

Fauvism was the first defiant movement in the 20th century. The name, given to the group by a Paris art critic, is derived from the French words *Les Fauves* meaning *the wild beasts.* The strongest characteristic of the Fauvists was their bold—and often garish—use of color. Precise drawing gave way to simplification and to color-conveyed emotion which appeared *wild* to the critics. Fauvism was short-lived, but it served as a stepping-off point for many famous artists who then went on to Cubism or developed their own individual styles. Georges Rouault painted religious subjects in colors separated by heavy black lines resembling the lead of stained glass windows; Raoul Dufy's toned-down colors seemed to express delight in a deft, highly personal style. The greatest of the Fauves, Henri Matisse, achieved great harmony and brilliance of color in a concise and economical style that often expressed joy in life.

Fauvists Painters

Henri Matisse 1869-1954
Andre Derain 1880-1954
Raoul Dufy 1877-1953
Maurice de Vlaminck 1876-1958
Georges Rouault 1871-1958
Albert Marquet 1875-1947

Henri Matisse
Dance (First Version)
The Museum of Modern Art

Pablo Picasso
The Pond in Horta de Ebro
Coleccion Particular, Paris

Cubism

The Cubist movement led by Picasso and Braque began in France in 1907 and lasted until about 1920. It still influences contemporary art. Throughout history all painters have had to deal with the problem of portraying a three-dimensional world on a flat two-dimensional surface. The Cubists' solution to this problem was looking at a single image from many aspects and putting all the aspects on one canvas in a geometric arrangement of blocks, lines and angles. For example, they often portrayed a full face and its profile at the same time, sometimes overlapping the face with other parts of the body so that the finished product suggested motion. In addition to the human figure, the Cubists also used objects as their points of departure—violins, guitars, bowls of fruit, etc. Because of their preoccupation with form, the early Cubists played down color, often using neutral shades of brown, gray or tan. Their emphasis on form, rather than subject, gave modern art its great push toward abstraction.

Cubists Painters

Pablo Picasso 1881-1973
Juan Gris 1887-1927
Fernand Leger 1881-1955
Francis Picabia 1878-1953
George Braque 1882-1963
Marcel Duchamp 1887-1968
Robert Delaunay 1885-1941

Abstract Art

Purely abstract painting was initiated by Wassily Kandinsky in Munich in 1910. The Abstract artists decided to give up the long tradition of painting real things, scenes or people. Instead they used colors, lines, patterns and other effects which produced no resemblance at all to natural objects or persons. This sharp break with the past required viewers to learn to look at paintings as combinations of form and color or as graphic representations of emotions or moods. Although it started in Europe, some of the most significant abstract painting has been done in the United States in what is called the New York School. See American Painting page 87. There are two main currents of Abstract Art:

Geometric Abstract Art is characterized by straight lines, logical patterns and geometric shapes. Some European abstract artists are:

Piet Mondrian 1872-1944
Kasimir Malevich 1878-1935
Antoine Pevsner 1886-1962

Piet Mondrian
Composition, 1921

Non-geometric Abstract Art has no definiable patterns. It is spontaneous and emotional compared to the carefully planned design of geometric abstracts. Its irregular appearance, sometimes resembling the drawings of children, often seems to convey either suppressed or impetuous feelings. Some European abstract painters are:

Wassily Kandinsky 1866-1944
Paul Klee 1879-1940
Kurt Schwitters 1887-1948
Hans Arp 1888-1966
Max Ernst 1891-1976
Joan Miró 1893-1983
Ben Nicholson 1894-1982
André Masson 1896-
Jean Dubuffet 1901-
Karel Appel 1921-

Joan Miró, *Woman and Little Girl in Front of the Sun*, Hirshhorn Museum Washington, D.C.

Surrealism

Surrealism began in Paris in 1924 and continued through the 1930's. Greatly influenced by Sigmund Freud, the Surrealists explored their subconscious minds and based their paintings on dreams, hallucinations, fantasies and symbolism. They often used real images in distorted or unreal settings in their efforts to put on canvas the secret life of the mind. Closely related to the Surrealists and included with them in this manual are the Fantasy Artists—particularly Marc Chagall who greatly enriched painting with his colorful, topsy-turvy, fairy-tale-like canvases.

Surrealist Painters

Salvador Dali 1904-
Joan Miró 1893-1983
René Magritte 1898-1967
Yves Tanguey 1900-1955
Max Ernst 1891-1976
Marc Chagall 1887-
Georgio De Chirico
  1888-1978
Paul Klee 1879-1940
André Masson 1896-

Marc Chagall
Green Violinist
The Solomon R. Guggenheim Museum
New York

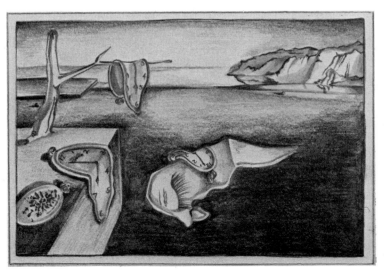

Salvador Dali
Persistence of Memory

Expressionism

Influenced by the horror of World War I, the Expressionist painters portrayed anguish and torment of the spirit. Their art was a reaction against what they felt was the unreal serenity of Impressionism. Using powerful distortions and harsh, violent colors, they attempted to portray man's troubled inner soul rather than the physical world they saw with their eyes. Expressionism had its roots in the work of El Greco and Van Gogh and it developed powerfully in the paintings of the Norwegian, Edvard Munch. Expressionism flourished as a movement in Germany in the early part of the twentieth century.

Primitive or Naive Painters

Primitive painters are usually self-taught artists who use a simple naive style for painting portraits, landscapes, many-peopled scenes and historical events. The word *naive* means showing natural simplicity or being without experience and information. Because they lacked formal training and familiarity with the works of recognized artists, these painters often omitted the shadows and gradations which usually give dimension to objects on a canvas. Also, they did not use perspective to relate the different items in a scene to each other. Nevertheless their paintings are direct and sincere and many of them show a masterful use of color.

Individual Primitive artists are found throughout art history. They were not a group working at a particular time in a particular place. Some of the artists' names are not known, even though their works hang in museums. The most famous Primitive artist is Henri Rousseau, whose work was discovered by Picasso.

Franz Marc, *The Gazelle*
Rhode Island School
of Design Museum

Expressionist Painters
James Ensor 1860-1949
Edvard Munch 1863-1944
Alexei Jawlensky 1864-1941
Emil Nolde 1867-1956
Paul Klee 1879-1940
Ernst Ludwig Kirchner 1880-1938
Franz Marc 1880-1916
Max Pechstein 1881-1955
Karl Schmidt-Rottluff 1884-1976
Oskar Kokoschka 1886-1983
August Macke 1887-1914

John Bradley, *Little Girl*
National Gallery of Art
Washington, D.C.

Primitive Painters
Henri Rousseau 1844-1910
Edward Hicks 1780-1849
John Kane 1860-1934
Linton Park 1826-1906
Horace Pippin 1888-1946
Grandma Moses 1860-1961
John Bradley active 1832-1847

AMERICAN PAINTING

The history of American Painting is a panorama of many different styles, some of which reflect those used in Europe. Unlike the Europeans, however, American painters had no demand for the palace scenes and religious subjects favored in Europe. They worked under the patronage of a middle-class society, and they painted their own people in familiar scenes of everyday life.

Pre-Colonial Years
The earliest painting in the land that is now the United States was done by the Native Americans, often as decorations on pottery. These artists used colorful earth tones to make intricate designs which sometimes had a zig-zag pattern. Their paintings also featured birds, animals, heads, headdresses, etc. Completely free of the tradition of Christianity, these **Native American** artists used their own unique symbols to reflect the Great Spirit which they believed inhabited all of nature and influenced their personal lives.

17th and 18th Centuries
Portraits done by the early European settlers in the seventeenth century were **Primitive** in style and those of the early eighteenth century were copies of styles used in England. However, in the mid-eighteenth century four famous native-born artists developed their own styles of painting portraits and scenes rather than imitating those of Europe:

    Benjamin West 1738-1820
    John Singleton Copley 1738-1815
    Charles Willson Peale 1741-1827
    Gilbert Stuart 1755-1828

Gilbert Stuart
George Washington
Sterling and Francine Clark Art Institute
Williamstown, MA

19th Century
Much of the painting in nineteenth century America featured the **Romantic** style because people who wanted to escape from their everyday lives enjoyed scenes of faraway places. Artists of the **Hudson River School** portrayed realistic landscapes in an idyllic manner:

Washington Allston 1779-1843
Samuel F.B. Morse 1791-1872
Asher Durand 1796-1886
Thomas Cole 1801-1848
George Inness 1825-1894
Frederic Church 1826-1900

But not all nineteenth century people enjoyed the romantic escape into a perfect dream world. Many were fascinated with the everyday world around them portrayed by the **Realists** (also called **Genre Painters**). These included:

William Sidney Mount 1807-1868
George Caleb Bingham 1811-1879
Winslow Homer 1836-1910
Thomas Eakins 1844-1916

Meanwhile some artist adventurers travelled west to paint the wilderness, the wildlife, the unspoiled Rocky Mountains, cowboys and the Native Americans. Some of the **Western Painters** and their subjects are:

John Audubon 1786-1851 birds
George Catlin 1796-1872 Native Americans
Albert Bierstadt 1830-1902 mountain scenes
Frederic Remington 1861-1909 cowboys and horses
Charles M. Russell 1864-1926 cowboys and horses

Winslow Homer
The Boat Builders
Indianapolis Museum of Art

Naive painting continued in the nineteenth century with the work of several artists of whom the most famous was Edward Hicks, 1780-1849.

In the late nineteenth century several American painters used the **Impressionist** style popular in Paris:

James McNeill Whistler 1834-1903
Mary Cassatt 1845-1926
William Merritt Chase 1849-1916
John Singer Sargent 1856-1925
Childe Hassam 1859-1933

Frederic Remington
The Cowboy
Amon Carter Museum, Fort Worth

Mary Cassatt
The Bath
The Art Institute of Chicago

88

20th Century

Twentieth century American art offers a rich variety of styles. In the early years a group called **The Eight** painted very commonplace subjects that were often rejected from the traditional exhibitions. Because of their depiction of the seamy side of life, they earned the nickname of **The Ash Can School**. However, this term belies the beauty of many of their paintings. The most well-known of *The Eight* were:

Maurice Prendergast 1859-1924
Robert Henri 1865-1929
George Luks 1867-1933
William Glackens 1870-1938
John Sloan 1871-1951
George Bellows 1882-1925 (associated with *The Eight* but not a member)

Because the United States is such a large country, **Regionalism** has always been a strong force and remains so today. Some Regionalist painters who used homegrown subject matter were:

Thomas Hart Benton 1889-1975
Grant Wood 1892-1941
John Steuart Curry 1897-1946

Some twentieth century American **Realists** are:
Edward Hopper 1882-1967
Rockwell Kent 1882-1971
Charles Burchfield 1893-1967
Norman Rockwell 1894-1978
Andrew Wyeth 1917-

With the coming of World War II many artists fled Europe and **New York** became a major center for contemporary art. The names **Abstract Expressionists** and **New York School** are used to describe many modern American artists, even though they have little in common with each other. Some who use compulsive movement are:

Stuart Davis 1894-1964
Willem de Kooning 1904-
Hans Hofmann 1880-1966
Robert Rauschenberg 1925-
Jackson Pollock 1912-1956
Larry Rivers 1923-
Mark Tobey 1890-1976
Roy Lichtenstein 1923-

Grant Wood
American Gothic
The Art Institute of Chicago

Robert Rauschenberg
Summer Rental, Number 2
Whitney Museum, New York

Others focus on all-pervading color:
Barnett Newman 1905-1970
Mark Rothko 1903-1969
Morris Louis 1912-1962
Sam Francis 1923-
Helen Frankenthaler 1928-
And still others offer geometric designs:
Josef Albers 1888-1976
Ellsworth Kelly 1923-
Frank Stella 1936-
Kenneth Noland 1924-

Pop Art is another twentieth century American style which portrays everyday objects, such as soup cans, in a very realistic manner. The most well-known Pop Artist is Andy Warhol born in 1928.

The mid-twentieth century American artists have not yet stood the test of time. Some of them will hold a significant place in the art history to be written in the future; others will be forgotten or recorded as only minor artists. The 1960's and 1970's in American Art have been crowded with many different types of painting competing for attention, such as Pop Art, Op Art, Conceptualism and Photo-realism. It remains for history to decide if any of these movements will ever become an actual school.

Mexican Art

Of all the modern nations in North and South America, Mexico has the oldest and richest artistic heritage. Beautiful pottery, sculpture, architecture, and wall paintings survive from a variety of highly developed native cultures which flourished in Mexico during specific periods from ancient times until the spanish conquest in the sixteenth century. Then Western-style art with its predominantly Christian themes was widely used to decorate churches and other public buildings. A wave of nationalism began with the Revolution of 1910 and three great muralists—Rivera, Orozco and Siqueiros—gave dramatic expression to strong political and social themes. Modern Mexican murals with their emotion-packed subjects and rich colors rank as some of the most famous in the world.

Andy Warhol
4 Campbell's Soup Cans
Leo Castelli Gallery

José Orozco
Zapatistas
The Museum of Modern Art, New York

Mexican Painters

José Maria Velasco 1840-1912
Saturnino Herŕan 1887-1918
José Clemente Orozco 1883-1949
Diego Rivera 1886-1957
David Alfaro Siqueiros 1896-
Rufino Tamayo 1899-

ORIENTAL ART

During all the years that Western Art was developing, Eastern or Oriental Art was flourishing in China, Japan, Persia and India. The style of Oriental Art is entirely different from Western Art because it developed under the influence of Buddhism and never portrayed the predominant subject matter of the West—Christianity. Oriental paintings exhibit very soft colors and delicate details. Their exquisite beauty influenced many Western artists of the 19th and 20th centuries.

18th Century Chinese
Flowers and Birds
Bibliotheque Nationale, Paris

Chinese Painting

Chinese art showed a development of style unbroken for over 2000 years. Ideas and styles were repeated over and over again; very few motifs were ever lost. That is why it is often difficult to distinguish a very old Chinese painting from a more recent one. Some of Chinese artists' greatest achievements were the landscape paintings done on scrolls. In a scroll painting, all the details are drawn into a wide vista which stretches out like a scene one sees from a passing car. Slowly a viewer turns the scroll, uncovering one part at a time from the right to the left and looking at what is almost a moving picture. Chinese landscape painters worked with ink on silk or paper, never able to erase any mark. Scroll artists also depicted animals and human figures such as mothers tending their children in a variety of activities. Chinese paintings are dated according to the dynasty or rulers at the time they were painted. The Chinese calligraphy which appears on many scrolls usually tells the story of what is portrayed by the artist.

Japanese Painting

Travelers from China to Japan in both the 8th century and the 15th century greatly influenced Japanese artists, teaching them the style of Buddhist painting and the technique of using ink on silk. From this beginning, the Japanese developed their own subjects which included battle scenes, humorous events in everyday life, and caricature such as animals behaving as pompous human beings etc. In the 17th century the Japanese needed imposing decorations which could be easily moved about in large castles or fortresses. A group of painters designed handsome screens, each with six panels, depicting people or scenes in intense flat colors. Even today Japanese screens decorated with paintings are some of the most beautiful screens in the world. Japanese painting is usually more simple than Chinese. It is interesting to notice how the Japanese developed the idea of blank space as part of their overall design.

Ogata Korin, Japanese painting, Edo Period
Freer Gallery of Art, Washington, D.C.

Index of Painters With Pronunciation Guide

The painters listed below are those whom you are most likely to encounter as you develop your postcard collection. For easy reference, the names by which the painters are most commonly known are arranged alphabetically. Wherever necessary, a name is followed by its pronunciation. Each painter's given name or surname is also included, followed by his or her dates and nationality. Page numbers are added only for those painters whose work is further described elsewhere in this text.

E

Eakins, Thomas 1844-1916
American, 88
El Greco, original name: Doménikos
Theotocopoulos 1541-1614
Greek, worked in Spain
54, 79, 86
Ensor (*en'·sor*), James 1860-1949
Belgium, 86
Ernst, Max 1891-1976 German, 85

F

Fantin-Latour (*fan·tin lä·toor'*), Henri
1836-1904 French
Feininger, Lyonel 1871-1956
American
Fragonard (*fra·gō·när'*), Jean-Honoré
1732-1806 French, 21, 54, 80
Francis, John 1808-1886
American, 52
Francis, Sam 1923- American, 90
Frankenthaler, Helen 1928-
American, 90

G

Gainsborough, Thomas 1727-1788
English, 54, 80
Gauguin (*gō·gan'*), Paul 1848-1903
French, 32-33, 42-43, 83
Gentileschi (*jen·tē·less'·kē*),
Artemisia 1597-1651 Italian
Géricault (*zhä·rē·kō*), Theodore
1791-1824 French, 81
Ghirlandaio (*gēr·län·dä'·yo*),
Domenico 1449-1494 Italian
Giotto (*jot'·tō*) di Bondone
1266-1337 Italian, 77
Glackens, William 1870-1938
American, 89
Gorky, Ashile 1904-1948 American
Gossaert, Jan 1478-1533 Flemish, 78
Gottlieb, Adolph 1903-
American
Goya (*goi'·ə*), Francisco de
1748-1828 Spanish, 65, 79, 81
Greuze (*grüz*), Jean Baptiste
1725-1805 French, 80
Gris (*grēs*), Juan 1887-1927
Spanish; worked in France, 84
Gros (*grō*), Antoine Jean 1771-1835
French, 81
Grünewald (*grü'·na·valt*), Mathis
1475/80-1528 German
Guthrie, James 1859-1930 Scottish
30-31

H

Hals, Frans 1580-1666 Dutch, 79
Harnett, William 1848-1892
American
Hartley, Marsden 1877-1943
American
Hassam, Childe 1859-1933
American, 88
Henri, (*hen'·rye*), Robert 1865-1929
American, 89
Herrán, (*er·rán*), Saturnino 1887-1919
Mexican, 90
Hicks, Edward 1780-1849 American
54, 86, 88
Hobbema (*hob'·ə·ma*), Meindert
1638-1709 Dutch, 79
Hofmann, Hans 1880-1966
American, 89
Hogarth, William 1697-1764
English, 54, 80
Holbein (*hōl'·bīn*), Ambrosius
1494-1520 German, 78
Holbein (*hōl·bīn*), Hans, the Younger
1497-1543 German, 78
Homer, Winslow 1836-1910
American, 88
Hopper, Edward 1882-1967
American, 89

I

Ingres (*an'·grə*), Jean-Auguste
Dominique 1780-1867 French, 81
Inness, George 1825-1894
American, 87

J

Jawlensky (*yâh·lĕns'·key*), Alexei von
1864-1941 Russian, 86
Johns, Jasper 1930- American
Johnson, Eastman 1824-1906
American
Jordaens (*yôr'·dans*), Jacob 1593-1678
Flemish, 78

K

Kandinsky (*kan·din'·skē*), Wassily
1866-1944 Russian, 85
Kane, John 1860-1934 American, 86
Kelly, Ellsworth 1923- American, 90
Kent, Rockwell 1882-1971
American, 89
Kirchner (*kirsh'·nər*), Ernst Ludwig
1880-1938 German, 86
Klee (*klā*), Paul 1879-1940 Swiss,
85, 86

Kline, Franz 1910-1962 American
Kokoschka (*kə·kosh'·kə*), Oskar
1886-1983 Austrian, 86

L

Larsson, Carl 1855-1919 Swedish
Lawrence, Thomas 1769-1830
English, 54, 80
Léger (*lā·zhā*), Fernand 1881-1955
French, 84
Leonardo da Vinci (*lē·ə·när·dō
də·vin'·chē*), 1452-1519
Italian, 54, 77
Leyster, Judith 1610-1660 Dutch, 79
Lichtenstein, Roy 1923- American, 89
Lippi (*lēp'·pē*), Fra Filippo
c, 1406-1469 Italian, 77
Louis, Morris 1912-1962 American,
90
Luks (*lukes*), George 1867-1933
American, 89

M

Macke (*mä·ke*) August 1887-1914
German, 86
Magritte (*mä·grēt'*), René 1898-1976
Belgium, 30-31, 85
Malevich (*ma·lə·vitch*), Kasimir
1898-1935 Russian, 57, 84
Manet (*má·nā'*), Edouard 1832-1883
French, 82
Mantegna (*män·tä'·nyä*), Andrea
1431-1506 Italian
Marc, Franz 1880-1916 German,
40-41, 86
Marin, John 1870-1953 American
Marquet (*mär·kā'*), Albert 1875-1947
French, 83
Masson (*ma·sôn*), André 1896-
French, 85
Massys (*mäs'·sīs*), Quentin
c 1466-1530 Flemish
Matisse (*mà·tēs'*), Henri 1869-1954
French, 65, 83
Memling, Hans 1435-1494 Flemish,
78
Metsu, Gabriel 1629-1667 Dutch, 79
Michelangelo (*mē·kəl·än'·jə·lō*)
Buonarroti 1475-1564 Italian,
46-47, 54, 77
Millais (*mil·ā*), John Everett
1829-1896 English

Suggested Art Books For Children

H.W. Janson with Samuel Cauman,
History of Art for Young People,
Harry N. Abrams, Inc., New York, 1982.

Ariane Ruskin,
Story of Art,
Pantheon Books, New York, 1964.

Ariane Ruskin Batterberry and
Michael Batterberry,
Story of American Art
for Young People,
Pantheon Books, New York, 1976.

Mary Lawrence,
Mother and Child, 100 Works of Art
Thomas Y. Crowell Company, New
York.

Ernest Raboff,
Art For Children Series,
Doubleday & Company, Inc.,
New York

> *Frederic Remington*
> *Henri De Toulouse-Lautrec*
> *Paul Klee*
> *Pierre Auguste Renoir*
> *Vincent Van Gogh*
> *Pablo Picasso* (out of print,
>   check local library)
> *Rembrandt Van Rijn* (out of
>   print, check local library)

Library of Fine Art
Woodbine Books, New York, 1980.

> Wendy Shore,
> *Major Styles in Modern Art,*
> *German Expressionists, Sym-*
> *bolism and Surrealism,*
>
> David Gillerman,
> *Northern Renaissance,*
>
> Alison De Lima Greene,
> *Romanticism and Neoclassicism,*

Ten Schools of Painting Series, National Gallery of Art, Washington,
D.C.

> *American Painting*
> *French Nineteenth Century*
>   *Painting*
> *Early Italian Painting*
> *French Painting of the Sixteenth-*
>   *the Eighteenth Centuries*
> *Flemish Painting*
> *Later Italian Painting*
> *Dutch Painting*
> *British Painting*
> *German Painting*
> *Spanish Painting*

Great Artists, Ladybird Books,
Hutchinson Books, Inc., Lewiston,
Maine,

> *Rubens, Rembrandt and*
> *Vermeer*, Book 1
> *Leonardo da Vinci, Michelangelo*
> *and Raphael*, Book 2
> *Van Gogh, Gauguin and*
> *Cezanne*, Book 3

About the Author

To make learning exciting for young children has always been an objective of Aline Wolf's professional work. Her concern for quality education for her own nine children led her to the work of Maria Montessori in 1960. The following year she and her husband, Gerald, founded Penn-Mont Academy, the first Montessori school to be licensed in Pennsylvania. Mrs. Wolf served as the first administrator of Penn-Mont. From this point of departure she began writing books, designing posters and compiling slide sets which focused on the type of environment and adult-child relationship which she felt to be most nourishing for a young child's development.

A graduate of Marywood College, Scranton, Pennsylvania, and the St. Nicholas Training Centre for the Montessori Method of Education, London, Mrs. Wolf lectures for parents and educators and has been an adjunct faculty member of the University of Pittsburgh and Pennsylvania State University.

About the Illustrator

Janine Sgrignoli Wolf holds a bachelor's degree in Art Education from Indiana University of Pennsylvania. During the past eight years she was an art instructor in the Harrisburg, Pennsylvania, public schools where she specialized in teaching pottery and batik to junior and senior high school students. Her art work was chosen by the state of Pennsylvania for its Women in the Arts Exhibit in 1982. Janine, who also performs with a modern dance group, has recently moved with her husband, Patrick, to Durham, North Carolina.

**Other Books by Aline D. Wolf
available from Parent Child Press**

The World of the Child
A fable for parents enabling them to experience what it feels like to be a very young child. Illustrated by Anna Marie Magagna.

A Book About Anna
A photographic picture book to read to toddlers or pre-schoolers about a precious little girl and the tasks she does every day with her family.

Look at the Child
Significant insights from the writings of Maria Montessori combined with photographs of young children in everyday situations.

Tutoring Is Caring—You Can Help Someone To Read
A complete manual for helpers who are not trained teachers.

A Parents' Guide to the Montessori Classroom
Complete description with photographs of Montessori materials for 3 through 6 year-olds. (Also available in Spanish).

About the Designer

Joan Stoliar is the award-winning designer of *Jonathan Livingston Seagull* and *Illusions* by Richard Bach and numerous other works by authors as diverse as James Clavell, Jorge Amado, Johnny Carson and Wanda Landowska. From her own design studio in Greenwich Village, she freelances for many of the major publishers. Ms. Stoliar has worked toward establishing copyrights for designers and holds the first copyright granted for a book design. She is design director of C.O.P.E. Book Design/Production Workshop at Cooper Union and lectures frequently for publishing audiences. Joan and her husband, Arthur, are the parents of a daughter and a son who are pursuing careers in the arts.

Pre-arranged sets of postcards to be used with each of the steps in this manual have been prepared by the author. For ordering information send a stamped self-addressed envelope to **PARENT CHILD PRESS
P.O. Box 767
Altoona, PA 16603**